the LIFE *of Your* CHOICE

the LIFE *of* *Your* CHOICE

Moving from *"Oh, No!"* to *"Oh, Wow!"*

DANIEL BAX

NEW YORK

the LIFE *of Your* CHOICE
Moving from *"Oh, No!"* to *"Oh, Wow!"*

Disclaimer: The Publisher and the Author make no representations or warranties with respect to the accuracy or completeness of the contents of this work and specifically disclaim all warranties, including without limitation warranties of fitness for a particular purpose. No warranty may be created or extended by sales or promotional materials. The advice and strategies contained herein may not be suitable for every situation. This work is sold with the understanding that the Publisher is not engaged in rendering legal, accounting, or other professional services. If professional assistance is required, the services of a competent professional person should be sought. Neither the Publisher nor the Author shall be liable for damages arising herefrom. The fact that an organization or website is referred to in this work as a citation and/or a potential source of further information does not mean that the Author or the Publisher endorses the information the organization or website may provide or recommendations it may make. Further, readers should be aware that internet websites listed in this work may have changed or disappeared between when this work was written and when it is read.

ISBN 978-1-61448-313-7 paperback
ISBN 978-1-61448-314-4 eBook
Library of Congress Control Number: 2012937526

Morgan James Publishing
The Entrepreneurial Publisher
5 Penn Plaza, 23rd Floor,
New York City, New York 10001
(212) 655-5470 office • (516) 908-4496 fax
www.MorganJamesPublishing.com

Cover Design by:
Rachel Lopez
www.r2cdesign.com

Interior Design by:
Bonnie Bushman
bonnie@caboodlegraphics.com

In an effort to support local communities, raise awareness and funds, Morgan James Publishing donates a percentage of all book sales for the life of each book to Habitat for Humanity Peninsula and Greater Williamsburg.

Get involved today, visit
www.MorganJamesBuilds.com.

Habitat
for Humanity®
Peninsula and
Greater Williamsburg
Building Partner

To my mother, **Shirley Wright**.

Your strength, loving care, and dedication made my rebirth possible.
Without you, this book would never have had a chance at life, and neither would I.
Raised twice by the same loving mother—wow!

TABLE OF CONTENTS

PREFACE

Dear Reader,

This book is a pragmatic, literal guide, not a hypothetical or theoretical discussion. It is for people who need and want healing and guidance in the mental, emotional, physical, and spiritual world. This book is also for people who have a passion and desire to get much more from their reality, to live life and not merely exist, and to learn how to create better outcomes consistently. If you believe there is much more to life than you have experienced, then this is the first day of the rest of your new life, because this is the book you've been waiting for.

As you apply these principles consistently to your life, you will quickly begin to experience the benefits. Re-creating your own reality will enable you to live in harmony and vibrate in resonance with the desires and dreams inside you. When you choose to live by these principles, your marvelous mind will expand exponentially to a place where you can create the reality that manifests your desires.

I wrote this book to show you how to expand and open your mind to all the possibilities around you. My intent is to encourage you to believe that you can accomplish all your goals, and this book is your guide on the journey to achieving them. The information in *The Life of Your Choice* is presented in a way that will reveal the abilities you already have within you to make all your dreams reality. One of the biggest realizations you may have in this book is that sometimes, to gain an entirely new perspective on any particular situation, all you need to do is ask different questions.

This is a very simple plan, but when lived, it will take you from where you are to where you really want to be. It may seem too simple, as though there must be a catch. But the catch is, there's no catch. This is real, and it is outstandingly effective. By consciously living the principles presented here, you will re-create your life with astounding results. As you believe and take action, you will begin to experience amazing changes before you have even finished this book. That is my word and my guarantee to you.

May you experience an inspiring and prosperous journey, and may your life be enriched beyond measure through your application of these principles. Many are now living the life of their choice. There is plenty of room for you to join them.

Your friend,

Daniel J. Bax

ACKNOWLEDGMENTS

Thank you, Lord, for all the daily blessings, for this new life and for the wonderful people you have brought into my world. Thank you for giving me a purpose and for showing me a new way to live. Thank you for guiding me through the re-creation of myself.

I thank my family for all the time you have invested in me, for the patience you've had, and for your strong love. I know I've been a handful along the way, but your determination in seeing me through the challenging moments has been tremendous. Without you, I would not be doing what I am today, and this book wouldn't be possible. Whenever you need me, I'll be here for you.

Thanks to the amazing vibrant people who have made a physical and mental contribution to my rebirth. My rehabilitation team, beginning with the beautiful and powerful woman that held us all together and in order, Mary Jusdanis; her amazing sidekick Jennifer Bose; Patty Nixon with her loving mother-like qualities as she guided me through my tedious physiotherapy; Dee Sperry with her big sister-like qualities, she made my walk through rehab worth speaking of; Dr. Bruce Baxter for guiding me through my wild and feisty thinking, providing the methods to have a clear balance throughout my days; Mrs. Heidi Anne Taylor, thank you for your patience and your drive to see me succeed and grow.

Thanks to my transitional living team directed by Mr. Paul McCormick, the guidance and ongoing assistance I received from your team was tremendous, the living elements I learned from you all has left an enriching impression upon me forever. Last, and most certainly not least, Jenny Rae for providing me with the freedom to move through releasing the intense muscle tension and knots I had riddled throughout my body. I could fill a page between therapist and surgeons; you all have left a tremendous impression of gratitude upon my life. If it were not for each and every one of you coming into my life when you did. I wouldn't have had the opportunity to learn what I needed to so I could move forward in life as far as I have.

I give deepest thanks to the outstanding leaders who have come into my life. You have taught me things that cannot be found anywhere else other than through experience. A special thanks to Brendon Burchard, for being the tremendous man you have become and for having patience and belief in me. You are paying forward the hope and possibility—some of what I have learned and continue to learn from your leadership. Brendon, you are a light to many people, and this opportunity to work with you is a highlight in my life.

Thanks to the person at the helm of deciphering this book into legible terms, Lorraine Phillips. How you did it, I'm not sure! I know you have spent countless hours with the initial scatterbrained drafts I began with, and you put them into a format we could use to begin creating this book. I am very grateful for all I have learned from you, Lorraine. You are a magnificent human being.

Thanks to Robyn Hanna, for your time and initial editing of this book. I truly appreciate your effort and feel blessed to have you as my friend. You brought light to my words and helped me make my thoughts clearer.

Yvonne Oswald, many thanks for the generous use of your time and extraordinary talents in reviewing this book and in guiding me to use just the right word in just the right way.

Michael Carr, the man who dotted the "i's," crossed the "t's," and made this book an enjoyable read for everyone who picks it up. Your skill in aligning this book's knowledge will enrich and empower lives.

Frances Pierantoni, I am blessed and grateful to have such an amazing beauty come into my life. It is in the desire to be a greater, better man for you that I have raised my standards to a higher level and am continuously improving. I know that who I am and what I have accomplished, and will still accomplish, is possible because of you. Frances, you mean the world to me.

Thank you all for your amazing contribution to life, keep it up and never give up.

INTRODUCTION

The Ultimate Wake-up Call:
when you get the calling, call life in!

I'm delighted to have been given this opportunity to add to Daniel's wonderful work. As a trainer of NLP and hypnosis and a therapist who specializes in emotional trauma, I see miracles on a weekly basis and know just how powerful the mind can be. I met Daniel over a year ago at a Toronto Power Group meeting. His likeable personality and sense of enthusiasm were catching. He reminded me of my younger self, because I also recovered in the same way from a near death experience.

I was twenty eight and living in Rome, Italy, teaching English in an International grade school. Six months into the contract I began to feel weak and wobbly, tired and bloated. I was nauseous much of the time. I knew I wasn't pregnant, and put it down to working too much. I didn't go back to school after Easter. I couldn't get out of bed. Just to move my legs I had to concentrate on literally sending a message to them and hoping it would get there. To get to the bathroom took a herculean effort; usually on my hands and knees. I had contracted hepatitis and Lyme's disease at the same time and was taken to hospital almost comatose.

I remember vaguely looking at the clock and seeing that it was 2am. I was sweating, vomiting and heaving in the bed and could do nothing to help myself. Everything suddenly went silent. I found myself drifting up towards the ceiling and remember feeling energised again. I looked back and down and saw a woman lying sprawled across the bed. "She was so young" I thought. It was dark in the room and I seemed to be drawn up and to the left towards the ceiling. It was gentle and freeing after the weeks of agony I had endured. I became aware of a lady in white standing in front of me. She had a young man to her right. I heard her say, although she did not move her lips, "What do you want to do?" "What are my options?" I asked "You can stay or you can go." There was no judgment and no feeling that it was anything but my choice. My thoughts went to England, where my mother still lived, and I vaguely thought that it would be a pity not to be able to say goodbye to her. And then a clear thought came in more strongly than I ever remember having a thought. "And I won't get to do the job I was supposed to do." Everything went silently dark again.

Recuperation took months, and I remember sitting for hours just looking at my hand and willing it to move. It felt like my body was not connected to my thoughts any more. The doctors told me that I'd never recover fully. So, like Daniel, I decided to prove them not right. I went on a search inside for meaning. Today I am completely healthy and more active than most people half my age. I am a best-selling author and travel worldwide doing Keynotes and teaching.

Reading Daniel's book brought back memories of the proof of the power of focused intent. The shift in consciousness that occurred while in hospital and later at home taught me to live life on purpose and with purpose, with a sense of fun and enjoyment. I learned to remember the blueprint and align myself with its simple coherence. To claim life with both hands.

Daniel went through an interesting experience in that, because his brain was not yet fully functioning, he was only able to grasp thoughts for a few seconds at a time. This is truly living in the now! He discovered something wonderful though – when you live in the now there is no room for self-doubt. You find inner power and strength that motivates you to be the best you can be. It gives you the freedom to accomplish the impossible. Most importantly, the lessons in this book will teach you that the projections of others are not valid unless they are succeeding where you are not.

Thomas Edison said that if we did all the things we are capable of, we would astound ourselves. We need to find out for ourselves how to connect with the inner workings of our minds and how to apply them to bring us daily fulfillment, happiness, health and prosperity. It's also important to discover what makes for a well-spent life – physically, emotionally, mentally and spiritually. Life is at its best a study of relationships – to self, to higher purpose, to others, and to God, or whatever label we give to the higher power that directs the plan. Because there is a plan - of that I am sure.

The Amazing Power of the Mind

Your own mind is the most powerful device available to you. It is millions of times more efficient than any computer and is your very own genie in the lamp. It is the Holy Grail that the ancients used to search for; a storehouse of inner knowledge and resources that are waiting to be discovered. Your brain is the interface between your mind and your results. It was during the late nineteen sixties that scientists made discoveries that seemed to indicate that the brain was not fixed as was previously believed. Pathways could be redirected through another route if one part of the brain was not working well. Coined neuroplasticity, this new discovery began to emerge as a scientific breakthrough.

Norman Doidge wrote in *The Brain that Changes Itself,* "I met a scientist who enabled people who had been blind since birth to see, another who enabled the deaf to hear; I spoke with people who had had strokes decades ago and had been declared incurable, who were helped to recover with neuroplastic treatments." (2007).

There was another concept that was challenged in the nineteen seventies. It was originally thought that the brain passed information through and was connected to the central nervous system electronically, like a wired telephone exchange. In 1972, Candace Pert's research into the ancient biochemical link between the physical body and emotions led to her discovery of the opiate receptor, which completely transformed neuroscience. She realized that awareness, beliefs, expectations and consciousness are translated on a biological level through the chemical interaction of peptides and their receptors, stimulating neuropeptides in a sequence, making instant connections. This multilevel exchange of information acts like a holographic matrix by passing information simultaneously and instantly to every system in the body. Ancient practitioners and shamans have known this for millenniums. The proof was finally here; that the mind and the body are one.

Lead a sunshine life

Happiness is possible when determination and honest intent lead to taking action and then trusting God. The continuous process of self-improvement that Daniel displays in his thinking and actions following his life-changing experience led to his mastering of authentic enthusiasm that displays his strength of character.

Understanding and being able to direct our minds on every level will allow us to have access to the amazing storehouse of untapped resources that will lead us to immense joy, purposeful living and inner peace. Happiness is achieved by staying constant in our inconstant world, and being proficient in self-direction is the highest form of self-actualization. People are ready to discover what is truly important. Go ahead and read The Life of Your Choice now to develop a new way of thinking, open up to bring happiness into your daily reality and find connection and meaning to life. It is time to reach your full human potential and love your life in oneness and joy.

Yvonne Oswald
MHt MNLP

A STORY UNLIKE
ANY OTHER

Life brings you what you ask of it. Thoughts equal actions, actions equal outcomes, and outcomes equal your destination in life. So…what are your thoughts?

This is my personal account of that wild day in the fall of 2005 when I made decisions that would change my life forever. Here is how it all began.

At the time, I thought life was great. I owned two businesses that were growing fast. I was achieving my goals, and I was involved in mountain bike competitions and other outdoor adventure sports. I decided one day to take one of my clients' motorcycle for a test ride. Thinking to stay away from traffic, I rode down country roads. I was taking preventive measures to protect myself from injury and to keep from damaging the bike. These precautions were important because I ran two businesses, but truth be told, I felt untouchable. I felt in supreme control of my actions. I just didn't remember that the universe will play into all that you think on and speak on—it will *bring* it on.

As I was riding down the back roads, I came up on a line of cars in front of me. Wanting to get away from them and get myself back into a safer environment, I proceeded to pass a row of six cars, through an intersection at the crest of a hill. Everyone knows, you don't do this. And you *especially* don't do this while on a motorcycle. As I was passing these six cars, the front vehicle, a van, made a left turn. It was still a good distance in front of me, but as I attempted to weave around it I was going so fast, the bike started sliding the moment I hit the brakes… so I slammed into the back of the van.

My left shoulder slammed into the rear panel support pillar of the van, pushing it in twelve to fourteen inches. When my head smashed through the back window, the impact shattered my left hand and left knee, split my tibia vertically, crushed my brachial plexus (the nerve network originating in the neck and controlling the hand, wrist, and shoulder), and collapsed my left shoulder. The momentum from hitting the van dragged me through the window. Shards of glass sliced open the left side of my neck, severing the *sternocleidomastoid* muscles, jugular vein, vagus nerve, and all the other arteries and tendons, all the way to the esophagus. According to onlookers, I was then tossed straight up into the air, *over* the streetlight. As I came down, I landed on my face, smashing my lower jaw wide open, breaking most of my molars in half, and knocking out a tooth. I fractured my neck at the first four cervical vertebrae, and my mid back was knocked out of alignment at the thoracic vertebrae T6 through T8. As if that weren't enough for one day, I lost four out of five liters of blood—two liters in my lungs and two liters in the ditch—and my brain endured anoxia for thirty minutes, from the moment of the accident until I got to the hospital.

One of the onlookers called the police. The police said they were rarely in the area, but they just happened to be two or three minutes down the road. The police called for EMS, who just happened to be on the highway already, and their next exit was the one leading to me. They were only five to ten minutes away from the accident scene, when normally it would have taken them about twenty minutes to get there. EMS then called for air transit to take me to the hospital, and although they are usually on a mission somewhere, that day they just happened to be flying above us when they were called. It seems God had it all figured out, and placed the units where they had to be to save my life. Apparently, my life's purpose had not yet been served.

I was in an induced coma. The record shows that I was a 3 on the Glasgow scale: "unconscious with no meaningful response and no voluntary movement." When I opened my eyes a week later, I was blind. The blow to my head was in a spot that affected my vision, which I slowly recovered later on. During this period, I was disconnected from the world, since I couldn't talk or see and didn't understand words. I lost all the skills I had learned since birth, so we can say I was a newborn trapped in a man's body. Definitely not good, right? But actually, this was far from being not good—on the contrary, having a blank slate was the door to my spiritual awakening. Since I had no concerns of any kind, I could listen to my inner voice. This is why meditation and silence are so important in our lives. Through silence, we connect to the Source, God, or whatever other name you may have for it. We just need to learn to listen to our spirit because, since it comes from the Source of Life, it has access to all the answers. This regaining of my connection to the spiritual realm is my most precious blessing. It was by listening to my spirit that I was guided through my healing journey.

The head nurse told my family that I was paralyzed on the left side of my body, which meant because of the paralyzed vocal cord, I wouldn't talk again or eat solid foods. I was sitting in a wheelchair right beside him when he said this. I looked at him and said in my mind (because I was still mute from the paralyzed vocal cord), "I'LL BE FREE. No one and nothing can ever hold me back. God created me, and God will heal me!" My grandma, Cora, was the only one who stood up for me, because the rest of the family was still in shock with the news. As if she were listening to my thoughts, she said to the nurse that he didn't know me and that she knew I would heal and do all those things he just said I wouldn't do again—just wait and see. And before that, while I was still unconscious, I also had friends coming to visit me and telling me how they believed I would heal. My brain didn't understand their words, but my spirit did. My family and friends would constantly play positive and motivational CDs from Anthony Robbins. This helped to reprogram my thoughts and beliefs.

At that time, I couldn't move or feel my left side. As I became more conscious, I began to focus all my energy on wiggling my toes. I would focus on this all the time when I was awake. One day, my mother came in, and as she was washing me I pointed at my foot. She looked. Nothing happened. The fear of failure briefly rushed through my body. So I pointed again, and sure enough, I could wiggle my toe! I had been working on this for days to surprise her, until I finally did. Just because you try something a few times and don't succeed doesn't mean it's time to throw in the towel. You never know how close you are to success. Just as Thomas Edison said when he was working to invent the lightbulb, "I have not failed. I've just found ten thousand ways that won't work." So did I—I tried until I found a way to make it work.

> **Be ever grateful for the very least of things,**
> **and the very most will come to you.**

Four months later, I was moved to a new hospital and they asked me my goals. I said, "I will walk out of here within one year!" They told me those were high hopes and advised me to get realistic. About six months later, I was walking, and I made it my goal, when I left the hospital, to leave them the cane and the wheelchair I was using. Once I started walking again, I went back to the first hospital, where I was treated for all my injuries, to thank the surgeon, nurses, and practitioners who had taken care of me and who thought I would never recover. (And who could blame them, having seen me in such bad shape?) I walked in using the wheelchair as my support.

When the surgeon saw me, he backed up. You could almost hear his jaw drop. He called for the rest of the team who had worked with him on my case. They couldn't believe their eyes! That moment, seeing the joy and wonder on their faces, made me feel more grateful than I had felt in years. And it's my hope that I inspired them that day to have more faith in what we, as human beings, are capable of achieving with perseverance and belief. I consider myself successful if their vision of healing and recovery opened up wide enough to encourage other people in their care never to give up. That's why I went back to thank them and show them I was able to overcome a bad medical prognosis with their help and care. I wanted to change the way they see their profession. I knew that I must fulfill my purpose in this life through encouraging the professionals in the medical industry. And when I succeed, many people under their care will benefit more and will avoid unnecessary suffering because of limited beliefs imposed on them about what they can achieve.

Since my rebirth, I realize that I have a mission and a purpose in this life. I had a calling, and I was procrastinating because my life was too busy and things were working out okay for me. It was because I was ignoring my mission in life that I hit a truck. It was my wake-up call. The years following that rebirth were really tough. They were also immensely fulfilling. That's because I was finally open to listen to the same inner voice that had been telling me all along what my purpose was: to share and spread inspiration, possibilities, guidance, and hope to as many people as I possibly can.

I endured thirty-four surgeries in thirty-six months, and between six and ten hours of rehabilitation daily for three years. Now, five years later, I am living independently. I re-create my life daily to live up to my purpose and higher values. I get to inspire and coach many to reach for the stars, break down all barriers, set new boundaries, and call into their life what they dream and desire. Now I am talking, walking, eating solid foods, and exercising using my left side daily. Nothing can or will ever hold me back from achieving my dreams and goals. I am opening up brand-new frontiers and setting new and higher standards for my life. Nothing will hold me back.

I must step up, step up, STEP UP!
—Anthony Robbins

I hope this challenge moves and stimulates you to become all you can. Allow your imagination to run wild to create the Life of Your Choice. You are worthy of all you desire!

Live with purpose; give with purpose.

Note from the Author:

This book is meant to help you accomplish your goals. To achieve them, I suggest picking one goal to focus on as you go through this book. Each chapter has four parts: explanation, example, experience, and exercise. It's vital that you complete each exercise before moving forward into the next chapter. Take as much time as you need to do it. The reason for this is that each chapter builds on the previous one. So take as much care building the foundation of your future as you would with the foundation of your house. Achieving many small goals will build up your skills and self-confidence to tackle bigger goals.

PART I.

AWAKENING YOUR GOALS AND DREAMS

Chapter 1

MIND-SET

Let's begin by defining "mind-set." For the purpose of our journey together throughout this book, when we talk about "mind-set" we are referring to the set of beliefs you have that affect the outcome of all your endeavors. Or, if this helps you clarify it, mind-set is also a fixed mental attitude or disposition that predetermines how you will interpret and respond to situations. In other words, your mind-set determines your outcomes!

Of all the things in life you have ever attempted without success, if you had the chance to try it again with a changed belief and mind-set, success would be in your own hands, and your outcome would be substantially better. As you become aware of your mind-set and learn how to use it to your advantage, you will find yourself succeeding in everything you undertake! So... interested?

How are you going to start your new life? By changing your mind-set! In this chapter, you'll take a look at some ways that have helped me do this very thing. Once you get the hang of it, you'll start coming up with your own methods.

The first thing to remember is that by changing your thoughts, you change your emotional state. Change your emotional state, and you will change the way you act and, therefore, your outcomes in life. Thoughts lead to emotions, emotions lead to actions, and actions lead to outcomes. Outcomes design your life. This is how you get to choose your life!

Ask yourself the questions below, and answer them honestly. There are no correct or incorrect answers. Take all time you need to write down the answers to the following questions:

- What is it that you would most like to change in your life?
  - » Something in your personal life?
  - » Something in your professional life?
  - » Something in your relationships with people around you?
- How important it is for you to make this change? Why?
- What are your current thoughts regarding those things you would like to change?
  - » Within your thoughts, what are the probabilities for the change to happen?
- Identify the themes of those thoughts.
  - » Do they have a similar pattern?
  - » Do they represent how you act in front of others?
  - » Do they point you in the same direction as your goals?
  - » What effect do they have on your motivation to act?
- How do these thoughts make you feel?
  - » How do they affect your mood?
  - » How do they affect your energy level?
  - » What is your physical response to these thoughts?

Your answers are going to be your starting point, the result of your old way of thinking. They do not define who you are now, and most certainly not who you will become. You are already a changed person. I know this because you are holding this book in your hands, and are now motivated by your desire and intention to change your life. How radical or subtle this change will be depends completely on your determination and how open you are to change at this moment. There is nothing wrong with being who you are, any more than there is anything wrong with a piece of carbon. But under the right conditions, that piece of carbon can be turned into a diamond. And you can turn yourself into the best you can be. This is YOUR life. Own it! None of us can change the things that happen in the wider world around us. We cannot change people or the past. What we CAN do is change ourselves—change our perceptions, responses, and attitudes. And in turn, all those changes will alter everything around us, as well as our own outcomes.

From now on, as you wake up every morning, think of your marvelous self, of your magnificent life and all you will accomplish during that sliver of it that is today. Even though you may think your life is not as great as you'd like right now, begin creating with your thoughts the life you would like to live. Think of the way you plan your day. Mentally, walk through your day even before your feet touch the floor. This will help you gain focus and guidance toward your goals and will help you to avoid living life by default. Start your day off by complimenting yourself. Begin your daily words with "I am . . ." and then follow by stating what you want to see and feel in yourself, and who you would like to become. For example: "I am feeling fantastic," "I am extremely happy," "I am successful," "I am grateful," "I am completely healthy," or "I am completely healed." In the beginning, you may feel as though you aren't telling yourself the truth, because you may not feel like the person you are describing. In those moments, just remember that the first step in becoming who you want to be is to think, feel, and act as if you already were that person. Everything begins with a thought. All thoughts are the seeds of something. Declare what you want out of life, and put your renewed mind-set to work. If your life is like a building, your thoughts are the blueprints—the design from which you build your life. Now you have the chance to change that blueprint to anything you want it to be! Now is the moment to become aware of the thoughts that will determine how you feel and how you act. Take those unsupportive thoughts that are not taking you forward towards where you would like to be, and replace them with supportive thoughts that give you options and open a world of opportunities.

Start creating your future in your present, thinking of ways you want events to turn out and what you would like to achieve in your life, rather than dwelling on things you don't think you can accomplish, become, or change. If you don't like the outcomes you have received thus far, there is something you can change within you to receive different ones. The question here is, how far are you willing to go to get what you really want? There is nothing you can do about the past. What you CAN do is to work in the present.

> ***All that you think about and speak about, you bring about.***
> **—Napoleon Hill**

When you are working toward what you wish for, if, after several attempts, you see no change or progress, change the questions you ask! If you've been asking, *Why can't my coworker be nicer to me?"* ask instead, *How can I be nicer to my coworker?* It isn't why something happens to you that matters; it's *what* you are going to do about it. Ask yourself how you can make things better, how you can see the lesson to be learned, and how this experience is going to make a difference in your future. Ask better questions, and you'll get better answers. You will not go through something that you do not have the strength to overcome. That strength is within you, and only you can find it and summon it in the moment of hardship. Asking better questions will enable you to view the situation from a different angle, get a new perspective, and create an entirely new outcome.

Ask yourself, *Am I living or merely existing? Are my actions moving me toward where I want to go? Am I doing what brings fulfillment and joy into my life? Am I experiencing life to the fullest?* These types of questions will have better answers as you pay attention to what you do with your time. When you think of something that needs to be done, ask yourself, *Is this helping me advance toward my goal?* Then rate it on a scale of 1 to 10, with 1 representing unimportant things that can wait or can be delegated; and 10 the things that are vitally important to do and should be done immediately. When rating the tasks or actions, rate them with the first value that comes to mind. If you take time to think about it, chances are that you won't assign the right value to it, because you are rationalizing the situation. As Nike says, "Just do it!" It's the first thought, the first feeling of how it rates in importance or significance, that counts. So don't try to reevaluate the same thought again—you'll just be changing the truth of its placement in your life.

The purpose of rating tasks, events, and actions is to help you decide how to invest your time wisely. Invest time in yourself, in high-quality activities, in your health, in your mind, in your spirit—in things that will enrich your life and put you in a mind-set to achieve greater things. This will bring you new energy, new vitality, and greater experiences. It will make you stronger in every facet of your life, be it mental, physical, emotional, spiritual, or social. You will begin to resonate with your dreams and ambitions. This doesn't mean you don't go out and have fun with life. It just means that by taking charge of what you consciously think about and do, you will automatically make your life more fun and worthwhile.

It's unfortunate that many people go through life not learning how to stand up for themselves, living instead by others' opinions or by what the media and conventional "wisdom" tell them. Every person has an innate desire deep within to become a better human being, and each of us has the individual responsibility to follow that desire through to completion. Begin to manage your conscious thinking by visualizing and imagining your journey's path with consistent focus. Your thoughts will make you feel better. When you feel better about yourself, you want to take action. And by taking action, you will change the course of your life. This translates into a harmonious life, which increases the clarity of your passions, dreams, and goals. Using visualization consistently will start a miraculous movement that aligns you with the law of attraction. As we said at the beginning of this chapter, it's all in the mind-set.

What do Beethoven, Anthony Robbins, Brian Tracy, John Maxwell, Marc Victor Hansen, Helen Keller, Terry Evenshen, Brendon Burchard, and many other great human beings have in common? This: that even though they may face hard times in different areas of their lives, they have always, continuously, created a life for themselves by their intentions. They've learned from their mistakes, from the mistakes others have made, and from the obstacles they have found in their paths, and they have become stronger as they figured out ways to accomplish their goals, and they kept on going. They have looked at every challenging moment as a learning experience, and found ways to become successful, better people. These are lessons you cannot learn unless you have experienced challenges personally. Their choice to face their challenges and always move forward comes from their mind-set.

Example

I'd like to share with you a short story about Gloria Estefan. In 1990, Gloria was on tour with the Miami Sound Machine when the bus she was in crashed and left her critically injured. She fractured her back and needed two titanium rods implanted to hold her spine in place, and she spent a very painful and difficult year between physical therapy and surgeries. Everyone thought her career was at an end, but she reappeared on the stage a year later with the new single "Coming Out of the Dark."

What do you think was the driving force behind her living life to its fullest before and after this life-changing challenge? How do you think she overcame this major hurdle in her life? It wasn't just good luck, or because she had some money, that she was up walking and performing so soon after such a devastating injury. She called into her life the strength she needed to heal, because she had her thoughts set on recovering and continuing with her life. She couldn't walk after the accident. She was young, she was told she couldn't have children, and her career was rising fast—how do you think she must have felt when she saw herself lying in a hospital bed? She fought the fight of the champions, and she won. After just a year, she was back on track, performing at a world-class level! What kind of mind-set do you think she had?

Experience

I literally had to experience death to realize my purpose and full potential in life. This was a double death. The first death was physical—I had to be resuscitated at least three times. The second one was that I had to die to my previous lifestyle. This is not the same for everyone, but it was necessary for me, because I was too stubborn to listen to my inner voice when it said, *slow down and take a look around.* Before the accident, I felt indestructible. Nothing would stop me from doing anything I wanted, even if it wasn't good for everyone involved. If someone told me I couldn't do something, I did it twice just to spite them. This included plenty of things most people would consider irresponsible or dangerous. It didn't matter to me, because I felt I wouldn't die doing it. I might get hurt, but nothing would stop me. I was invincible! I had a somewhat cocky attitude, you might say. Uh… *somewhat?* I was full of myself! Three earlier accidents had almost claimed my life in the previous three to four years, not to mention the goofy stuff I did as a kid, which could have killed me many times over. Can you see how I would believe that I was bombproof? Having survived as many brushes with death as I did, I grew cocky in my thoughts and actions.

Don't do this at home, boys and girls! You, either, ladies and gents! It is not a good character trait to have. Just because you make it by the skin of your teeth a few times is not some divine sign that you always will. No. What it actually means is, if you don't change your ways now, the end is near. I know, through personal experience. The accident was as close to death as one ever gets to come back from. I flatlined at least three times on the operating table. I was in an induced coma for ten days. My new mind-set was chosen before I came out of my coma. My family often played Anthony Robbins CDs as I lay there. This was one of the greatest things they could have done for my recovery. The CDs reached deeper into my subconscious than I knew. This affected my mind-set in every way. The continuous positive messages on those CDs were ingrained into my brain and developed me into the person I am today. I still listen to them and read self-improvement and personal development material daily to keep in this mind-set and create this state. I chose and I choose to live life completely in every sphere, not just to exist in the world. I choose to give back to life multiple times for all I have ever taken or been given. I will assist and guide anyone—physically, emotionally, mentally, or spiritually, to overcome his or her challenges. Giving unexpectedly and unconditionally without demeaning anyone or myself, in my every venture in this new life, brings me great pleasure and joy.

EXERCISE

During your day while you're at home, working, or just going about your daily routines, pay attention to where you are not having it easy, or what you may be getting stuck on. Take a moment and look for ways you could alter your thinking on any particular point to get an outcome that serves you or others involved.

NOTHING HAPPENS BY ACCIDENT

Chapter 2

Not a single thing in your life ever happens by accident. Everything is brought about by thoughts, feelings, and actions. The results that you are experiencing in your life come from your actions, and these results will have the same characteristics or qualities as the thoughts that created them. Have you ever thought about someone and felt you needed to call that person? Then, when you do call, the first thing that person says is, "I was just thinking about you!" What happened was, your thought's vibration was sent out to the universe (*I should get in touch with Dan*), and the universe answered back (*Dan called you*). This happens all the time, in everything you do—you just don't usually notice it. What we need to do is *become aware* of this fact.

The images that you plant in your mind instantly set up an attraction energy. This energy is the one that governs the outcome of your actions while creating the life you are experiencing. This doesn't mean that the results are always the ones we want, only that the attraction works the same for everything. Continuously switching the thoughts of what you are or what you want to become makes the process chaotic. How often have you said something like this: "I can't afford that"; "I just can't seem to get rid of this cold"; "I'm such a klutz!" These are negative or low-vibration thoughts. By doing this, you are defying the law of growth. Just know that the law always works by providing what the vibrations ask. If you are consistently changing your vibrations by attracting positive or high vibrations in one moment and, the next moment, neutralizing it or attracting the opposite, this causes the attraction energy to vibrate out of harmony and into disorder, placing you in a spiral that slows you down.

Everything you strive for is also striving for you with equal intensity. Everything you desire is already yours to claim. All you need do is send out the vibration (an intense thought followed by an intense feeling, then action), and it will be returned to you as the physical manifestation of your desire. Once you become conscious of what you already possess, it becomes your reality. The secret to receiving more on a conscious plane is by truly understanding the six faculties of the mind. These are will, memory, reason, perception, intuition, and imagination. In this book, you will also learn another key factor in creating your life to be all you ever dreamed it to be: the understanding of how to get yourself into this harmonious vibration. As you practice it daily, you will come into a new understanding of how the things I've been mentioning actually work. It's one of those things you just have to experience for yourself. Once you start putting this to work for you, it will stir something so deep within you that the vibrations begin to manifest in your life even while you sleep!

> *The very best thing you do in the whole*
> *world is to make the most of yourself.*
> —**Wallace D. Wattles**

Example

All will go exactly as you think it will. Just hoping or wishing it all will turn out well only leaves you hoping and wishing. Believing and doing equals achieving. It is and always has been the way of life. Ask any of the greats.

Wayne Gretzky's efforts since childhood paid off as he moved his way up to the NHL. He started playing hockey when he was 6 years old, on a rink his father built. When he was 15, he had impressed scouts with his abilities. By the age of 17, he had represented Canada internationally. His dream was to join the NHL. He played in the league for the Edmonton Oilers, Los Angeles Kings, St. Louis Blues, and New York Rangers until he retired in 1999. When he retired after the season, the NHL retired his number, 99, to ensure that no one else would ever wear it. Gretzky played in the NHL's All-Star Game every year and was the first player to be named MVP with three different teams, and his teams claimed the title of world champions three times. And he got to realize another of his boyhood dreams when he was selected to represent Canada at the 1998 Olympic Winter Games in Nagano, Japan. In 2000, he was named executive director of Canada's 2002 men's Olympic hockey team. That was the year they ended a fifty-year Olympic drought for Canadian men's hockey teams.

The Great One's style was unique and almost impenetrable. He visualized the play before it was made or the puck was dropped. And he skated to where the puck was *going,* not where it had been. Why do you think he scored as many goals as he did? Yes, he possessed extraordinary hockey skills, but he also had the right mind-set and put the right thoughts in his head to *attract* success.

As you can see, he worked really hard for all this. He had practiced since he was a boy, and never quit. He pushed himself to be his best, and that took him to his dream: to be part of the NHL. It was all his own doing. It was a choice to live his life with purpose.

Do you think, after all the hours of training and the team transfers that any of this would have happened if he had just hoped for it without putting in the dedicated time? Do you think it was a coincidence that he accomplished and won just about everything there was to win in the hockey world? Did all his awards, rankings, and respect happen by luck?

Or would you agree that Wayne Gretzky might have been envisioning it all, just as he did with his puck handling? And he was backing it all up with a solid passion and fierce determination that made his heart beat stronger with every thought of how to reach his childhood dream. He has inspired many others along the way, touching the lives of people who were not even hockey fans.

Experience

Before the accident, I sometimes raced mountain bikes, both downhill and cross-country. At one practice, I was on a steep hill, with a log jump downhill and through the trees. All riders walk the hill before racing it, to learn what to watch for, so they can arrive in one piece at the bottom of the hill. I had watched others in past races tearing down this hill at breakneck speed. They would hit this log jump, soar in the air a long way down the hill, land in control, and keep rolling. Ribbons and cautionary signs are placed on the course to prevent accidents.

On this particular day, no caution signs were in place, since it was a practice day. My mind was focused on just enjoying the ride, so I hadn't walked the hill. I just expected everything to flow as I desired. Here is where, if you don't pay attention to the environment, the environment can control your actions and dictate the outcome. I flew down the hill, rolling smoothly along this trail, going faster after every corner and bigger on every jump, and thinking all the while, *damn, I'm good!* This trail was easy. In fact, though, reality was about to kick me in the face.

As I came around the turn, the big log jump was there. Moving along at a fast clip, I hit the jump, pulled up harder than I should have, and flew down the hill farther than I would have if I had been prepared and acting instead of reacting. When I landed, I went slightly off trail in the taller grass, where I nailed a tiny tree stump. Big or small, stumps don't move. Their roots go deeper into the ground than your tires do. With an abrupt halt to the bike's forward motion, I left it behind and kept right on going. I needed a bit of practice on my Superman landings—flew well, though the landing was a bit rough. I flew about thirty feet off my bike down the hill, landed on the back of my head, and collapsed like an accordion. This popped a hole into my bladder, and my spleen exploded like a water balloon.

Why did all this happen? No, it wasn't an accident, for nothing happens by accident! My lack of reasoning, perception, memory, and intuition—and the fact that I was living purely in the faculties of will and imagination—had promoted me to do what I desired now (short term) over what I wanted most (long term), which was a fun and smooth, fulfilling experience. What are your thoughts? Do you think this was an accident or a reaction? Ponder that for a moment!

> *The chief cause of failure and unhappiness is trading*
> *what you want most for what you want now!*
> **—Unknown**

Exercise

Whatever you desire to do, have, or become, begin today by looking into it deeper and more intently. If it's a job, what are the qualifications? Do you have them? If not, where can you get them, and how long will this take? What you are doing here is living life with purpose and intent. Dream build! Create a vision board to look at daily. This will help you visualize your dreams and will remind you, every day when you look at it, what kind of life you are creating for yourself.

Chapter 3

THOUGHTS
CREATE
THINGS

Any idea that is held in the mind that is emphasized, that is either feared or revered will begin at once to clothe itself in the most convenient and appropriate physical form that is available. Every thought you mentally entertain begins to materialize in your physical world the moment the thought enters your mind.
—Napoleon Hill

All the thoughts you focus or concentrate on will be generated into your reality in some form. They are created from the substance of life and the energy of thought. When you begin to think these thoughts with passion and detail, reality begins to form. When you see and feel the rush, recognize the emotion, and fully experience the thought in your mind you will be living it before it physically manifests. You don't dive into the specifics of how it will all come about. In the end, while keeping all possibilities open, you are not concerned with *how* you achieved, as long as you *have* achieved.

There are in the neighborhood of sixty thousand thoughts per day running through your mind. Let them flow freely in a constructive manner, without trying to guide or control them. There are too many; it would only confuse you and make you nuts. Focus only on the ones that are consistent and that you are conscious of. These are the more predominant thoughts that control your actions.

It's like this: thoughts create things, either constructive or destructive. If you keep in your mind thoughts of loss or lack, it's guaranteed that this reality of loss or lack will manifest. As I said, when you begin to think about something with passion, you begin to create it in your world. Constructive or destructive, it makes no difference to the higher energy. The universe just wants to bring to you all that you focus on. The more energy and action you put into this thought, the faster and more intense an environment of people, places, events, and opportunities will come into your life.

Thoughts are much more powerful than most people imagine. Small changes in thought and action can make a big difference in our lives.

Watch your thoughts; they lead to attitudes.
Watch your attitudes; they lead to words.
Watch your words; they lead to actions.
Watch your actions; they lead to habits.
Watch your habits; they lead to character.
Watch your character; it determines your destiny.
—Unknown

Example

Walt Disney is a wonderful example of thoughts creating things. In the beginning of his career, he found himself with serious challenges as he lost his animators and the rights to his animated character, Oswald the Lucky Rabbit. Yet he always kept drawing until one day he came up with a mouse named Mickey. His cartoons weren't a hit right away, and he had to keep trying until he sold one of his Mickey Mouse cartoons.

As his cartoons became more popular, Walt and his company started creating more characters.

> **If it can be dreamed, it can be done.**
> **—Walt Disney**

Walt Disney could have stayed with just making cartoons, but his creative thoughts took him on a different path. He decided to create theme parks and attractions, hotels, water parks…Well, he wanted to create a different world, and he did. By following his dreams of something bigger and better, he let his thoughts come to life. He thought, he felt, and he took action. Walt Disney passed away before seeing Walt Disney World completed, but he had already seen it in his mind.

Experience

Thoughts create things. Let's see one of the many ways this works. Shortly after the motorcycle incident, while still in the hospital, I was told I would never walk, talk, eat solid food, or move my left side again. The first thought was, *Is that a challenge?* My second thought, which gave even more power and energy to the first thought, was, *How dare you try to impress your limiting opinions on me or my family!* This fired me up to meditate ever deeper and get even closer with the Creator through prayer and paying attention to the guidance I received. This means listening, not just hearing or feeling the intuitions, but paying attention and acting on them.

I knew, and the thought had been bouncing around in my head that what had put me there was going to take me out of there, on my own two feet. Determination, faith, tenacious spirit, ignorance, and visualization would be my motivation. Yes, *ignorance.* Ignorance is the state of being uninformed, and so I decided not to know what I couldn't do. They said I couldn't walk, so I learned to walk; they said I couldn't talk, so I learned to talk. Now I talk enough for everyone! I also completely redefined in my mind the meaning of "ignorance." Its meaning went from not thinking, and running blindly through life, to a thoughtful self-study of where I was and where I was going from there.

I created all this by re-creating my mind-set to be at a higher vibration than what was expected of anyone with such severe injuries. I didn't belong here "in the hospital" for long, and I knew that if I was to get out I would need to accept where I was and all that I must do, however long it took me. There are a number of things my focused thoughts brought into my life at that specific time. I received most things I needed during the stays in the hospitals and rehabilitation centers. When I focused on where I wanted to go and whom I needed to work with or connect with, I found myself where I needed or wanted to be in a relatively short time. For example, I was the patient of some of the best, if not *the* best, doctors in Ontario who would work on my case. I would get the best physical therapists to improve my movement. The people who surrounded me would help me move toward my goals, even though they may have thought my goals a little too high and unrealistic. Because I believed in myself, they believed in me. They believed that I could make it, that I would walk, eat, and talk again. Of course, there were moments when people simply would not believe in what I wanted to achieve. In those moments, when they weren't as supportive as I would have liked, I simply listened to myself and moved forward. Soon afterward, somehow, someone else would come along who would help me achieve more. This is something I will always remember: how powerful focused, intentional thoughts are. I live by this principle. It's like a map to life; it will direct you down the path of your choice.

It's kind of fun to do the impossible.
—Walt Disney

I thought about the movement in my body and the feeling of it working in complete harmony with my right side. I thought about being able to walk, talk, and eat solid food, too. Every day, I would visualize walking as I went through the rehab program. First, I was able to move my toes, then the rest of my feet, then my legs, until I was finally walking. The same went for talking and eating food. This was a long process, but I knew it was going to be from the start, and most importantly, I knew what the outcome would be.

Eventually, what I said and thought consistently has come about. If you see me today, only a few years later, I'm living proof. I can walk; I can talk—too much, some people might say—and I feed myself solid foods, and my left side is at 90 percent and getting better.

Now that I've completed my rehabilitation in medical facilities, I find myself focusing on what it is I can do within and for this community. I want to give back to the medical professions and the people they serve, in acknowledgment of what I received during my time there. I have this unquenchable desire to share with everyone how we can achieve the "impossible." I want to share that I did it! I did all the "impossible" things I was told I couldn't! With thoughts of what I would like to do and whom I should connect with running consistently through my mind, I'm finding that everything is playing out just as I believe it will. I am meeting the people I need to meet, and getting the opportunities I need in order to place the right people around me.

My every move today is consciously thought before I make it. What has changed most is that now I think *before* making decisions that otherwise would have been spontaneous, with the potential of placing me in random, perilous situations. I also know much more about thoughts creating things than I ever did before the accident, and I have used this to create a more meaningful life.

> ***Believe and your belief will create the fact.***
> **—William James**

Exercise
What are you creating with your thoughts? Take a look at the answers you wrote down in the first chapter, and review what your thoughts about those things are like. If your thoughts are not constructive, positive, and

making you feel better about yourself and the situation, then you know what you've been creating for your life.

Let's take the following example. You wake up in the morning and do your exercise of going through your day in your mind—getting into details, feeling it, seeing it, and putting emotion into it. Then you get ready to go about your day, and someone (your spouse, your boss, maybe a stranger) comes along with an "interesting" attitude and turns your day upside down. It happens, right? This is what's really going on. But consider this: by letting other people turn your day upside down, you are just accepting their reality as yours. That's the challenge! It's like going from your house to the mall—if there is construction on the road, you can take the side roads, but your destination is always the same. From now on, create your day in your mind in the morning, and when you find a "detour" sign during the day, return as soon as you can to your day as you created it, and keep your own destination intact. How much better would your life be if *you*, not someone else, truly created your thoughts?

Now it's up to you to decide what will be the predominant thoughts running through your head. When you get a thought you don't like, replace it with one you *do* want. And do more than that: *speak it aloud,* just loud enough so you can hear it and repeat it three times. Hold yourself accountable and do this for a solid week—whenever you get a thought you don't want to hear or entertain, speak what it is you would like to hear, and repeat it three times. You have a greater say than you think in what thoughts you have running through your head.

Chapter 4

SEEKING

Seeking? Seeking what? Though often confused with *looking,* seeking is much more than just dreaming or looking for something. There is a difference between looking for something and seeking it out—a huge difference! Let's look at their definitions:

- *Looking:* to use one's sight or vision in searching, examining, or watching.
- *Seeking:* to go in search of or in quest of.

One of my mentors, Bob Proctor, said in *The Secret,* "All you are seeking is seeking you right back with equal intensity." When you believe in your dreams as intensely and confidently as your body seeks its next breath, you will truly understand the meaning of this phrase. Your body knows that air is there, that it will be available when required. No thought is necessary; it automatically knows what to do. Likewise, when you believe in your dreams, visions, and desires as strongly and naturally, you will be amazed at what and who comes to you.

It doesn't matter whether you "want" to manifest it. What makes all the difference is whether you're passionate about it. At this point, you may be thinking you are not passionate about what's going on in your life right now. Maybe there's this draining theme flowing through your life that you're not especially wild about. I agree that you may not be passionate about the negative or draining things, but the questions is, are you being passionate in the way you express yourself about what you dislike or don't want in your life? For if you are, you are expressing that dislike with the same intensity as if you desired or craved it. Either way, you're putting a strong vibration out to this universe, and that strong vibration is like a magnet, attracting what you're passionate about. Whether you love it or loathe it, want more of it or want it out of your life forever, you are calling it closer, drawing it into your life. Whether pulling on it or pushing it away, if you're doing it constantly and with passion, you are seeking it out. Let's suspend any lingering disbelief for a moment and take a closer look at your environment and your life, wherever you are. Does it represent what you think, feel, and talk about all the time?

You are always seeking something in life, whether you consciously know it or not. Have you heard the saying "things always come in threes"? This is because once something good happens, your thoughts will create more of it. The same happens if it's something chaotic. Your attitude and mind-set dictate whether it's positive or negative. Your history is all the proof you need to realize that the choices you have made brought you to where you are. Most importantly, your history is the reminder that all choices you will make from this day forward will direct you to where you are going to be.

So... once you understand that you are always seeking, it's best to be aware of *what* you are seeking in order to realize the goals and dreams you so desire. So how do you consciously put yourself in the state of being aware of what you are seeking? It's quite simple. Paying attention to your conscious thoughts is one of the key elements in knowing and understanding what you are seeking.

> ### *It is like this: thoughts become things.*
> **—Yogi Gupta**

It is crucial to have your destination in mind before you set out. If you get an idea to go traveling without a set destination or agenda, any road will get you there. You already have an idea—or even several ideas—of where you would like to go; you just aren't sure how to get there, because you aren't sure which destination to choose.

We've all said at some point, "I thought of doing that," "I was just talking about that," or "That's a place I dreamed of going for a long time." We didn't follow through with those things, because we didn't believe in them enough to *seek them out*. We didn't have a consciously chosen destination or outcome, so there was nothing to follow through on with action. The likely reason for this is that we didn't have a *desire* or a *passionate purpose* strong enough to drive us into action.

Having the drive to seek out your desires requires passion. You must know what you will do once you have obtained what you are seeking to its fullest. Knowing whatever it is you want out of this life is the key to creating and experiencing all that you want on this journey. A destination will give you a vision of where you are going, and your purpose will guide you to all that you are seeking.

Example

Mary Kay Ash created a revolution with her new approach to doing business. After many years as a salesperson whose work went unrecognized because of her gender, she wanted to offer women the same opportunities for success that any man enjoyed in the business world. So in 1963, with five thousand dollars in her pocket and with nine independent beauty consultants, she started her company. Today her company has more than 350,000 consultants and makes over a billion dollars in sales internationally. What characterizes her company are the values and priorities it was built on. Mary Kay always followed the Golden Rule, "Do unto others as you would have them do unto you," and her priorities were "God first, family second, and work third."

Mary Kay had her mind set on a destination: she wanted to give women the same opportunities to grow financially that men had. Not only that, she figured out a way to do it by encouraging women to grow personally and spiritually. Mary Kay's company was recognized as one of the hundred best companies to work for in America, and one of the ten best companies for women to work for. It received the Equal Justice Award, and Mary Kay was named the Most Outstanding Woman in Business in the 20th Century. I'm pretty sure she didn't expect for her new and innovative business model to be studied at the best graduate business schools in the country. And it all started with her seeking better opportunities because she didn't like how she was being treated in the business world.

> *I think it is good to remember that we don't sing because we are happy. We are happy because we sing. Try to make life lemonade even though you may be given only a lemon. Success is never an accident. It is always deliberate. Whatever your lot in life, build something on it! Be a risk taker. Don't be afraid to fail.*
> —**Mary Kay Ash**

Experience

The moment I first opened my eyes after the accident, I began seeking. As I grew conscious in thought and life again, I made it my purpose to heal my body and fulfill the mission I was given along with my second chance to live. I seek spiritual guidance through meditation and by being more connected to nature. I discovered that when I took walks barefoot on the grass, even when it was in the backyard of the rehabilitation facility, my body felt better, more alive, in less pain, and I felt a closer connection to my spirit.

I was seeking truth and life through all avenues. I still am! I have a powerful emotional desire and passion to experience life in every way humanly possible. I believe there are many more avenues than I am even aware of. I was completely open to finding myself. I had to find the purpose and meaning of my life, and it was a walk I was willing to take again.

Just as Mary Kay continuously sought better ways of doing business and promoting women's personal and financial growth, I went on a worldwide investigation of natural remedies to regain my health and mobility again. I was seeking out a spiritual energy that knew the natural ways of healing—more than just relying on pills and procedures. I'm talking natural holistic energy. I began to look for this life's energy after I felt the healing energy of the universe (or our Creator, as I like to call him). As God guided me, he had piqued my curiosity to find out every way one could heal and experience life to the fullest. I must say, it's been one heck of a stimulation, for it has defined my life's purpose ever since.

In seeking out the many different sources of life's energy, I have been fortunate enough to find many of them, and I benefit from them every day. I haven't always been wise enough with this vessel over the years, and certainly not before this session of rejuvenation. I needed to study how to help the healing and push it beyond what even the professionals thought possible. Then, to fulfill my purpose, it was a given that I must study these elements so I could teach them to other people. Only then could I connect with the leading rehabilitation institutions so that we as a team might design affordable ways to bring these wellness modalities to the public.

I'm going to share with you what I have found that truly works for me. As I mentioned, I spent a lot of time in silence and isolation from the world around me. During this time, all I had were my thoughts. In those moments of silence when I asked myself why I had to suffer and be confined to a bed, I heard a voice inside me that soothed and encouraged me. This inner voice advised me to have faith in my recovery and assured me that I would be completely healed if I did what I was asked to do.

Since I wanted to heal, I agreed to listen and follow the advice given to me. I found that the more I did as I was asked and the quieter I got, the better I felt, and the faster my healing progressed. In being asked, I knew the *foundational essence* of these suggestions and knew that they came from a higher power. And I knew that my healing depended on my heeding these suggestions. Feeling the energy, I knew it was a creative, constructive energy that could only guide me to heal. It was through the continuing meditation that I kept receiving the knowledge I needed, and that is how I was asked to fulfill my purpose in life: to help others. When I learned what I was supposed to do with the rest of my life, my quest to make it a reality began, and it has continued ever since.

Exercise

I will ask you, as I often ask myself to keep on track, what do you want from this life? What are you seeking?

The purpose of this exercise is to find your next destination and put you on your path toward it. At this point, you can be in one of three positions:

- You already know where you want to go with your life.
- You have more than one place you would like to go, and you haven't narrowed it down to one.
- You have no clue whatever, about what you want out of life.

The first step is to be in touch with your inner voice. I will suggest that you take time twice a day, preferably in the morning and at night, to meditate and to be in silence. You've probably heard or read about how to meditate, and there are plenty of resources out there that can give you several ways to reach a meditative state. All I ask you to do is to find a quiet spot where you can have at least ten to fifteen minutes to silence your mind. You could use some soft instrumental music if that helps. Sit comfortably, close your eyes, relax your body, and release the world around you, and set the intention of your meditation. Ask a question, such as *What's the purpose of my life? What should I do next to achieve my goal?* You can be as specific as you like with your questions, though remember that most of the time, we have no clue what our future holds for us or how we will receive it. It may take some time to listen to your inner voice. Keep on meditating until you do—it is one of the most exciting moments you can have in your life! Be aware that sometimes we wish for things that are not good for us, although we may not realize it. Your inner voice will know, so let it guide you into the fulfillment of your life.

IT IS AS YOU DESIGN IT TO BE

Chapter 5

Think of yourself as a master chess player and, at the same time, a chess piece in this beautifully abundant earth. Your purpose in life is to learn and grow while you enjoy the game, and it is also to win, achieving goals one after another until you have fulfilled your destiny in this life's journey. The universe has given you all you need—no more, no less. At this point in your life, you are given as much as you can handle and use for living an abundant life. You will be entrusted with more as you feel more grateful each day for what you do have and as you learn how to make the most of what you have been given.

From the moment of conception, you were endowed with a great ability, in every one of your faculties, to become whatever your mind conceives and believes. You have all the power and energy you will ever need to overcome adversity, break through, and grow into someone who is much more than you ever were before. Design your life, as you want it to be. Choose—and yes, you must make a choice—to be open and willing to design your future as you feel it manifesting.

Toss out those old unconsciously programmed thoughts of "I can't see myself being anything more than I am now," "I don't have an imagination," "I'm too old; my time has passed," "I don't have…," "I'm not…," "I would if I only had…" Do it again, this time with a new mind-set. Think of yourself as a vessel that God has created to work through and to serve a greater purpose on this earth. You have a life to live. This life is your own and no one else's. Don't allow others' opinions to create yours. If they don't live up to your standard, they shouldn't leave an impression on your thinking. You're worth far more than that.

Here's a thought for you. If your life isn't as you choose it to be, then what the heck is holding you back from making it more than it is? Habits? Old paradigms? If you're not happy or satisfied with what you have or are now, then why don't you step up and out of this mental bind and begin designing the life you have always desired? I know, it's not as easy as it sounds. But it's not easy living a life you don't like, either. You're spending more time wishing for something else instead of investing that effort and time in creating something that you will enjoy and deserve. If you could do just 5 percent or 10 percent of all the things you wish for, how mighty would your life be? Then what are you waiting for? When you believe in you and put yourself into motion, you can be all you have desired. Quit messing around. You are a magnificent piece of art and power!

Never submit to the possibility of failure or
speak in any way that sees it as a possibility.
—Wallace D. Wattles

Example

Gary Coxe started his first business at age 11 and his second at age 15, and by age 17 he was making a hundred thousand dollars a year. At this point, he was thinking of quitting school. I probably would, too! But here's where life turned around on him. He got married and had a child, his wife told him the baby was not his, his father was murdered, his grandfather and stepfather died of cancer, his uncle was killed in a plane crash, he lost thirty thousand dollars in savings, and his business making him a hundred thousand a year went under. All this happened in a three-year time frame, by the time he turned 21 years old.

Gary was an emotional wreck, on medication and, at times, drinking heavily. He hit rock bottom! Did that stop him? No! With his faith, a new mind-set, and a desire to move ahead from where he was, he started making strides. If he could be successful once, he could do it again.

He endured more trouble and heartache in three years than most do in a lifetime. He had fears of falling in love and of being around people. He was scared even to think of trying to succeed financially again, for fear that he would just lose everything anyway. And yet, step-by-step, he made changes and opened his curtains to let the light in. He changed his "friends" and got off his medication. He did all this with a mind-set that has stayed with him until this day. He certainly can say that moving forward is still often "easier said than done," but he persevered in designing his life as he wanted it to be.

You may be wondering, what has he done for himself after all he endured? Well, he began his new life by getting in front of people who wanted a change—people just like you. He decided to share his life experience through seminars and CD programs, he got in front of millions of people, and he saw that people's lives began to change. This led him into the world of self-development, and he found that he loved teaching and watching people succeed by applying what they have learned from his events.

This has brought Gary to a point where his life is quite a bit more exciting than if he had given up. Instead, he is living his life *as he designed it to be*.

Experience

Your life truly is and has always been as you designed it to be. My personal experience in designing my life as I choose it to be began with my rehabilitation and the re-creation of myself. After all the challenges

I've gone through, I have chosen to live my life out based on my own decisions, not on the opinions of others (unless a particular opinion looks worthy). The only opinions I will listen to are from people who are trustworthy, who have been there and conquered, or who are sharing information that I can learn something from.

The greatest pleasure in life is doing
what people say you cannot do.
—Walter Bagehot

I am booked to speak at hospitals during training days or in-services, and also at medical colleges and universities to share about communication and relations between health-care provider and client. This gives me the opportunity to leave my audiences with a deeper insight into human potential. To this day, I am still designing my own life experience, and part of this experience is to leave an enriching impact within the medical and rehabilitation community.

Nothing can stop the man with the right mental
attitude from achieving his goal; nothing on earth can
help the man with the wrong mental attitude.
—Thomas Jefferson

I have designed and created this life of mine through the experiences I have endured and my desire to improve the communication between patients and health-care professionals. My experiences have also led me to become the person I am today, with the vision to grow into the person I desire to be, with "constant and never-ending improvement."[5] I have chosen a life for myself that enriches, inspires, and guides many, and I have chosen to facilitate a movement that will flow through the medical and rehabilitation industry in North America and touch down all around the world.

People may say—and I can hear it very clearly—"You're a dreamer. It's impossible. What makes you think you can do this?" It is something I dream of daily, and with every breath I take, I have a passionate purpose and commitment to generate a greater understanding of the human potential throughout the medical world.

> *Do what you do so well that when others see what it is that you do, they will want to see you do it again, and they will bring others with them, to show them what it is that you do!*
> **—Walt Disney**

I am walking this purpose and living out my passion in life. Every day, I make another planned move and open a new door. As I see it, my life can go wherever I choose it to go, as long as I am determined to climb the obstacles and make stepping-stones out of challenges on the path to success. I have chosen some great mentors. I'm constantly listening to their teachings through their CD programs, seminars, events, and books. My new goal is to work with them one-on-one.

I have also chosen to leave this world knowing I have benefited all whose paths I cross, as long as they are open to receive. I live every day to the fullest and look forward to encountering other ways to raise my standards in life still further.

"I can, I will, I must" go that extra mile. As I take the steps to plan out my life according to my desires, it can only become as I design it to be. I take consistent action in the creation of my life. From the moment I wake each day, I thank my Creator for giving me another day to serve others and life.

> *Do what you do so well that when others see what it is that you do, they will want to see you do it again, and they will bring others with them, to show them what it is that you do!*
> **—Walt Disney**

Exercise

What is it that you long for? How does it fit in your life? How would you like it to turn out? Now it's time for you to start making things happen in your life. In chapter 1, you were asked to gather more information about something you want to change. It's your turn to make it a reality. The first step is to break down the big goal into smaller, achievable goals. For example, if you want to get a better, more fulfilling job, some achievable goals could be to create your résumé, make a list of companies you would like to work for, ask for job applications at those places, and find support on how to improve your skills for job interviews, to name a few. If you want to have a healthier body, then you can read books on nutrition, search for recipes for new, delicious healthier foods, find a friend to join you on a daily morning or afternoon walk, join a gym if you prefer, and fix that bike in the shed and start biking to work or to the grocery store.

What this does is break down that big goal, which could feel overwhelming or unachievable, into smaller pieces that you can get your arms around. The smaller they are, the better. Here's a trick: The lists I made for both examples are categories of the particular goal. Each category can be broken down into even smaller tasks. You want to write a list of those smaller tasks. The following is an illustration of what your list might look like if you want to make your home greener and friendlier to our planet by using more natural and nontoxic household cleaning products:

1. Search for recipes to make cleaning products at home.
   • Check in the bookstore and online for books on the topic.
   • Go to the library and look for available books on the topic.
   • Ask people I know if they have any recipes to share.
2. Research what ingredients are better.
3. Find out if any equipment is needed.
4. Find out how to store the products.

5. Are there any organizations that can offer more information?
   - Do they offer workshops or literature?
6. Search stores where I can get the ingredients.
   - Compare prices.
   - Can I get them in bulk?
   - Get stores' operating hours and days.
7. Go shopping for the products.
8. Select and write down a day on the calendar to prepare the cleaning products to use during the month.

Remember, the smaller the task, the better! If it helps, brainstorm with someone to help you make this list. Another person's point of view may enrich your list by coming up with tasks you didn't think of on your own, thus simplifying a task even more, or sharing some resources that could be useful. Ask someone who is already where you want to be, someone you trust who will offer support. Just do the best you can now; you can modify the list as you learn more. This list is your action plan, and you will use it in the next chapter.

YOUR MAGNIFICENT SELF

Our Lord has blessed us all with the gift to visualize and create. We are gifted with the ability to look at any situation and see far beyond whatever may immediately appear in our reality. We can take any challenge and focus on the obstacles it presents, or we can benefit from this opportunity and find ways to grow mentally, physically, and spiritually. It's time for us to focus on clear and positive objectives that will give us outstanding results.

> *Creative means believing that you have greatness.*
> —Wayne W. Dyer

You are a tremendously creative individual. You have a powerful mind that can make anything happen as long as you keep yourself centered. As you practice maintaining your magnificent self, you will refuse to play in others' games. Remember that someone else's behavior belongs to *that* person. That is their reality, and they created it for themselves. They are looking for actors to play a role in their reality, but so are you! You create your reality, too; we all do. You, too, are looking for actors to play a role in your reality, and only you assign the roles to everyone who comes into your life. As you understand this, the reality of another person should no longer affect you, unless you let it. If you find yourself being treated in a way that you resent or that turns you into a victim, ask yourself this question: What have I done to teach this person that this behavior is something I'm willing to tolerate? Remember that you choose the actors, you design your life, and you can be *anything* you want! So choose to become the magnificent being you are meant to be!

Three major parts of your magnificent self are your thoughts, feelings, and actions. Thought is a powerful intention, but you won't receive all you want and desire by thought alone. Through your thoughts and feelings, events and people are brought to you to assist you. By action, which is talking and walking those thoughts and feelings, you will manifest your creation. Without the work of your hands and feet, your thought will never turn into reality.

Here's an example, a story we can all resonate with. This can happen with anything you want. I just picked this example. You want a dog—let's say, a female golden retriever. Hold this thought in your mind until it's clear. Keep adding to it daily. See yourself walking with the dog, playing, petting it, feeding it, and grooming it. Hold it there with a clear, distinct mental image of how it will look, feel, smell, and sound. Have grateful faith that you are receiving the thing you envision. As you are putting time and effort into this vision, your reality transforms to accommodate your thoughts. When everything aligns, the opportunities to get your golden retriever will come your way, and then it's up to you to take action or not.

Thought:

You're wanting this dog, visualizing her in every aspect: playing with her, feeding her, and petting her. Feeling the emotions when she nuzzles up for some loving, imagine yourself laughing out of sheer joy at the silly and joyous acts she presents.

This thought is so intense; you can almost smell her at times. You're already missing the sound of her crunching her food as she eats; you're seeing her lie in her favorite spot as you watch TV or chat with guests at home. You must bring your thought to this stimulating, intense level, for you will generate an energy that will radiate from your body. You'll be amazed to find that everywhere you go, you attract dogs and owners walking their golden retrievers. It will occur so many times, it will stop you in your tracks. You will ask yourself why you didn't do this before—with everything!

Action:

You must talk about your dog as if she were already living with you. Get excited talking about the things you will be doing with her, driving with her around town, going for walks in the park, hiking adventures, giving her the last bit of your sandwich. Let your imagination run free. Let it go. It's not doing anything for you if you're keeping it captive in your head. Let it out NOW! Go to the dog park and watch the dogs, talk to the owners, visit the shelter, talk to breeders.

When everything in your reality aligns itself, it's then that you begin to receive it. As you're speaking to a friend, a relative, or a stranger in the park, they may ask, "What kind of dog do you want or like?" You let them know you want and will have a female golden retriever. Say it—I want you to say what you are wanting now. Say it out loud. As you are telling them, they say, "Wait a minute. I have a friend (or relative or friend of a friend) who can't take care of their dog anymore, and they want to send her (yes, *her*) off to a good home, not the kennel. They have a golden retriever with all the shots, leashes, bowls, food, travel cage, even toys, and they will let her go to a good home for free (or very little)."

Another key factor is that your vision must not be a selfish one. You must see greatness in your vision for all involved, knowing you will bring joy and fulfillment to anyone whose path you cross. It's far more enriching than receiving the bounty of the universe for yourself alone. There must be a greater good for humanity and nature in all that you create with your thoughts. What this really means is simply that you should want something for the *right reasons*. If you want to create a business, do it because it will provide a service to people. It is something that people need, it will make you richer in many areas, and it is your passion—it's not just something you're doing to make a bunch of money.

Summing this up, you can see how it works. You think certain thoughts, feel as if they are already happening, and the universe aligns itself, bringing the people and events to you to materialize it in your reality. What a remarkable creation you are! You were created to create! You are designed to be a magnificent self!

> *Ask and you shall receive. Search and you will find.*
> *Knock and the door will be opened for you.*
> —Matthew 7, 78

Example

Kyle Maynard is a champion athlete. During his senior year of high school, he was one of the top wrestlers in Georgia. He trains and competes in both power lifting and Brazilian jiujitsu and has fought in mixed martial arts inside a cage. Kyle is an entrepreneur with his own fitness center, and he also travels around the United States and the world as a motivational speaker, author, and model. What may seem most astonishing of all is that he accomplished all these things without having arms or legs below his elbows and knees, because of a rare disorder called congenital amputation. He doesn't use prosthetics, yet he has mastered eating with silverware, types fifty words a minute, and has impeccable handwriting. Kyle credits his family and friends for the love, encouragement, and support that helped him overcome his physical challenges and turn into the man he is.

He has truly sought out his magnificent self. It's a gift we all have been blessed with by our Creator at birth. The only difference between you and Kyle is how you are choosing to use your gifts and what you are choosing to focus on. I consider Kyle's most important lesson to be this: he overcomes his challenges by doing what gives him passion, and focuses on what works—and no excuses.

Look inside yourself and begin to awaken, to become aware of your talents and gifts and to realize how magnificent they are. Many people, like Kyle, have the potential to illuminate you and others. Let them inspire you, and make it your purpose to see others as what they are meant to be: magnificent beings like your own magnificent self. The potential inside the people who surround you is boundless. You can become a light of hope for others by leading them through your example. Your history doesn't matter; your future does. Focus on your future, on who you're going to become and what you will do with whom you are becoming.

Kyle Maynard's academic and athletic accomplishments are the fruits of what truly makes him an outstanding person: his faith, attitude, and perseverance. He doesn't think in terms of limitations, only in accomplishments.

> *It's not what I can do; it's what I WILL do.*
> —**Kyle Maynard**

Experience

I chose to make it my mission, in every moment of my new life, to give and uplift others, to guide and support those around me more than I ever did before. With this in mind, I've looked for opportunities to travel, connect, and network with new people who can guide me on my journey to fulfill my purpose of helping others who are going through those challenges I've been through. As I meet successful people, I also have the opportunity to learn from them. It's easy to see how magnificent these people are! They have accomplished so much and are happy to share their knowledge with others. You can tell that they know something not everyone has yet come to realize.

Through this new group of friends and mentors, I've come to see myself through a different lens. I can see how magnificent I am as well, even though I haven't yet achieved all the things on my list of goals. The secret is simply to see others for what they are and to appreciate what they can become.

I visualize myself accomplishing daily all I have ever dreamed of. There are some outstanding things I want to do in this world with the gifts I've been blessed with. I hold myself accountable for it all, and when I need extra support, I share with everyone I respect who also respects me for my vision. I would not want to let them down, and knowing that they hold me accountable for my goals moves me to do what I need to do to accomplish them.

This is why I aim to wow myself with what I can accomplish, whom I can connect with, and how much I can help people in need of guidance and support. By impressing myself is how I've come to know that I have grown. It also helps me tap into a higher vibration of energy. By doing things that were once a challenge, I prove to myself that I'm on the right track to transform into the magnificent self I was created to become. By wowing myself, I am shown all the possibilities in front of me, and I will know I'm on the correct course I have chosen for this life.

I thought I was good. I was stuck in my head and hooked on ego. And yet, I never realized how much talent, power, endurance, strength, and love I had in me, until this massive wake-up call. And now I get to live fully, experiencing all that I was ignorant of before. I just wish people wouldn't secretly seek out trauma before coming to the realization that we have all that we need here before us right now.

When I meditate or when I'm in a focused thought of creation, such as when writing this book, designing my next move for Daniel Bax Speaks, or working with my mastermind family on developing life, I take a few moments to visualize the outcome. I think of all the ways I could best benefit others and myself during the process. This is when I purposefully tap into my magnificent side and create what my spirit guides me to.

*We may think we are doing the right thing, but
the Lord always knows what is in our hearts.*
—Proverbs 21, 2

Exercise

What have you intended to become, change, or do in your life? Begin to think about it and visualize it with a powerful emotion and a descriptive desire. Take action on your intention. Get out and do something about it today, even if it is to dream about building or creating it.

Now is the time to take out the list you created in the last exercise and start taking action on each of the tasks you wrote down. You want your life to change; you want it to be different. So take a deep breath and jump into it. When I wanted to walk, I started by moving my toe. All it takes is a small step each time. Consistent small steps will take you a long way. Just pick one task at a time, and move on to the next when you have completed it. Avoid overwhelming yourself. This exercise will help you gain self-confidence and build the foundation for those moments when you will need to tackle bigger tasks, or more tasks in less time. Things will start to flow when you start moving toward your goals. Keep in mind your long-term goal, but focus on that small step you are taking right now. If you get frustrated or disappointed because that one small step "didn't work," remember that people don't become elite athletes overnight. The great news is that by taking that one small step, you are a lot closer to living the life *you* design than you were before you took it.

PART II.

UNDERSTANDING WHERE YOU ARE

STEP BACK

We often hear people say, "You just need to step back from it," or "I just need to step back for a moment to clear my head." When we hear people say this, do they mean *literally* to step back? What's the benefit of "stepping back"?

I found out that when most people use the phrase "step back," they mean to step back mentally, spiritually, or emotionally from a situation (although, occasionally, they may refer literally to taking a physical step back). Both refer to stepping back from your present situation and taking a look at it from another point of view, a different angle. When you gain a new perspective on the event, you can approach the issue with a clearer mind, which will enable you to succeed in your endeavor with greater confidence and focus.

How do you step back from a situation? When an issue seems overwhelming and impossible to resolve, your mind is in a state of chaos. Because you are so involved in the situation, it isn't easy to see a way to fix it. For example, say a man is standing in front of a wall. If his nose is against the brick, he can't see the height or length of the wall,

45

or a way around it. But if he steps back a couple of feet, he can see that that the wall has a top, and if he steps farther back, he can see that it has ends. This new perspective allows him to go around it, which was his purpose in the first place. Likewise, when you are immersed in a situation, you sometimes can't see a way out, because you're too close to it, either literally or figuratively. But taking a step back from it gives you a different view, allowing you to think of ways to resolve it.

Stepping back from a situation allows your mind to seek possible answers that aren't evident when you are buried in the challenge, so you can concentrate on finding new ways to move toward success. This will also give you a better sense of balance and place you in a higher vibration so that when you return to the challenge, you can move forward with a greater insight and determination to accomplish your aim.

Example

In 1971, Mr. W. Mitchell, age 28, was in a motorcycle accident in which the gas from his tank poured all over him and then ignited from the heat of the engine. In his words, "I became a human bonfire." Over 65 percent of his body suffered second- and third-degree burns. Four years later, while he was piloting his own plane, a crash landing left him paralyzed from the waist down.

This left Mitchell asking himself what he was going to do with this experience and how he was going to use it to do something greater with his life. When he took the time to step back and look at what he was consistently focusing on, he noticed a pattern. What came back through every action was his focus on all that was wrong in his life: how little he could do, how disabled and unattractive he was. Mitchell began asking himself better questions, and at the same time he began focusing on what he could do with what he had. Over the next two years, as he began to get feeling back in his body, he started to feed and dress himself, drive a car, and fly airplanes again. He decided to look at himself and his life from a completely different perspective. Mitchell began to focus on the gift that lives inside each of us, and on the people around him as well. In the process, he discovered that he was creative and had more strength within him than he realized.

For the first time in his life, he began to believe that he had choices. He took that step back, became aware, and began to understand that he was responsible for his own experience. No matter who was wrong and who was right, it was still him in the hospital, all messed up. It was his future, and he needed to take control of it NOW. He needed to be responsible for himself and his recovery. Responsible, as Steven Covey says it, is being *response-able*.

With the support of some newfound friends, he soon started building his life again. He began to design his new life as he saw it becoming. He started a successful business. Mitchell's indomitable mind-set, courage, strength of will, and gratitude for life allowed him to wage a fight against the world's largest international mining company to preserve the beauty and environment of his hometown. This time, Mitchell purposefully woke up his magnificent self to come to the aid of his town and fight for something bigger than himself. He has served two terms as the mayor of Crested Butte, Colorado, and has taken action on his passion to run for Congress. All it took from W. Mitchell was a step back to discover how he could move forward in his new passion for life.

Experience

This was a MUST-do, right after the accident: I needed to take a huge step back mentally and spiritually. When I woke up and realized what the heck had happened, I finally looked back at what I had done through life and where it had taken me. I questioned whether it was leading me down the path I felt comfortable with deep inside, and whether I felt true passion. This doesn't mean I didn't like what I was doing in my life at the time. I loved it, and I couldn't consciously conceive of a different path to walk. The keyword here is "consciously." Was I living my purpose, or was I just living a want?

My subconscious, or spiritual self, knew I should be doing something far greater with my life and not just walking through it with a singular focus on my business and fitness. So in this step back—well, more of an adventurous hike through rehab, really—I chose to listen intently to my inner self. You know that "voice in the back of your head" you sometimes listen to? It's more than just an annoying sound distracting you. As I began to connect and communicate with my spirit, I asked what my purpose was in this new life and how I should go about bringing it to my reality.

Just like W. Mitchell, I had no choice but to step back at this point! Not only did I have to start my life all over again, I had to decide whether I even wanted to and, indeed, whether it was worth it. Decision made. It was! So... how to do this? Looking back at the pictures of me before the accident, I needed to make a decision about whether I wanted to become that person again. What and who I saw in the pictures made me ask, did I want to do the work? And if I did, could I summon the energy to accomplish this monumental feat? And if I could and chose to, would it ever be possible to be anything like that physically or mentally again? Could my body and mind ever "do" life and live self-sufficiently again? Did I want to continue to leave that kind of impression on this world? Or did I want to improve myself, live my purpose, and leave a greater impression on every path I crossed?

> *Life is a unique combination of "want to" and "how to,"*
> *and we need to give equal attention to both.*
> **—Jim Rohn**

I believe it was the best decision I ever made. Being forced to step back, look at the situation I put myself in, and reevaluate made me recognize the person I was. It also gave me a vision of the person I had the potential to become. And that potential was far greater than anyone could ever have expected or imagined of someone in my particular condition at the time. Most people are not forced to step back, so they go about their daily routine uninspired, unsatisfied, robotic. This accident forced me to take another look, leaving me with an entirely new view of life.

My life changed completely in an eyeblink! One move by ego triggered one massive rebirth. When you're reborn at age 30 you can't get away with all the cute and funny things you did when you were 3. They are corny and immature when you're an adult. That wasn't fair at all, since my mentality was at about the level of a child. Everything my 2-year-old nephew said made complete sense. As adults, we make communication too complex!

One would think I had lost everything and had precious little to build on. I had no choice but to look at where I was going from here—and even *whether* I was going anywhere. Fortunately, the connection I had with our Creator told me I had a purpose. It was my choice to make this hard or easy on myself. I never said it's a simple or smooth walk through life. Difficulties and challenges are the platforms for growth, and a huge part of the plan of life. They bring new opportunities and adventures to your life and, at times, can be your compass.

From that place, I made the decision to walk, talk, and eat solid food again. Oh, yeah, I almost forgot: and to breathe on my own, without machines to keep me alive. All those functions of life that we generally take for granted were no longer a given.

Thanks in part to the Anthony Robbins CDs played to me while I was in a coma and continuously thereafter, I realized I wanted much more from this life. I wanted more than who and what I was before, and I knew that the first step was to get myself together and focus on healing. My purpose was very clear to me now. How I was going to manage it wasn't so clear, only that I had to. I had to share this life experience with the world. I had to give hope, to help others break through their challenges in life and keep on learning and growing from all they have experienced. I had now found my purpose.

I am guided to do for others as much as I do for myself. I have found it to be a process of giving while you are receiving, especially when it is done through love and joy. It is a smooth sort of blend: giving and receiving. For me, this means getting known publicly throughout the therapeutic facilities and hospitals I frequently visit. I am driven to help anyone I can, absolutely anyone! I will be the first to admit that I don't do everything perfectly. I just look at it as classroom experience, because I am always learning and always going for an "E" on my assignments— "E" for "effort" and "excellence."

What a tremendous feeling it is to have found your purpose and to know beyond any wisp of a doubt what path you are to walk. It's a lonely state not knowing why you are here and why you are doing what you're doing—especially if you don't *like* what you're doing. The journey I chose was to find out what I am supposed to do with my life— something fulfilling and valuable. I needed to go through an accident that nearly cost me my life, because I was too stubborn to step back and see all the messages, in large print on the wall right in front of me. The Spirit was the guide to the greater purpose I have found for Daniel J. Bax. The new walk in this world is to share the story of my journey with you and, possibly, to be a facilitator on your journey, to help you become all that you have ever dreamed of being. Please allow the bumps and bruises you have endured to serve as your compass in finding your passion so that you can fulfill your purpose in this life.

I chose to treat this particular step back as my schooling in communication, human potential, and the power of the mind. That has led me into the field of speaking and trauma recovery coaching. I knew that sharing with professionals and strivers would be a fantastic purpose for someone who had endured such a life-changing event. Having had to learn everything from the ground up again, I could speak with the voice of experience. This could be a tremendous service to offer, and it would bring joy and fulfillment to my life because it fit harmoniously with my new purpose! When I woke up, I had a choice, just as you do right now. I could choose to go back to being the person I was, or I could make a change and become who I dreamed of being, and enjoy all that I imagined. In hearing from my family and friends about the person

I was before, I found many different facets of him that I admired, but there were just as many things about him I didn't appreciate at all. So I chose to change, and the journey began. The most important step of making a change is actually to step back and look at your situation or circumstance and evaluate whether you choose to trudge back through it or leave it behind.

> *You cannot change unless you know what it is you want to change. You do not know what you want to change unless you step back, look at the situation, and evaluate.*
> —**Bob Proctor**

I found it nothing short of magical how things began to line up for me when I started to walk the path of my purpose and when I created actions that fit my vision. Instead of moving about without a definite destination or purpose—not settled or established. My every step was taking me further ahead, because I was in the right place at the right moment to meet the people who would mentor me. You may have experienced some of this aimless wandering when having to do the exercises from the past few chapters. If you haven't done them, saying to yourself, *I'll get to them later*, or *I'll do them when I have time*, there is no better time than now to create some new, stronger habits for yourself and step into the person you want to be or even think you would like to be. Dr. W. Edwards Deming said, "Your key to success is gradual, constant, never-ending improvement at an incremental level, by constantly improving the little things. Your quality of life will come together at a level most people never dreamed possible, but it must be daily, and it must be consistently."

Exercise

Step back. Take a step back from the situations or challenges that have been stretching you and wearing you down. Whether mentally, physically, or both, step back now. Don't think about it; don't speak about it. Take that break you've been wanting, even if it's only a walk to get a cup of tea or coffee. When you come back you will have a fresher mind, and you can come at it with a new perspective. This will let you perceive anew the challenge confronting you. The goal of this exercise is to gain a new perspective on a situation. You may need to repeat this a few times before you see that situation differently. To accomplish this goal, you may need to meditate or you may need to listen to someone with a different point of view. The more you practice this exercise, the more you will master it. This is an exercise for every situation, project, and challenge. Dare to think differently. Dare to be a different person. But first, step back.

Chapter 8 > SATISFACTION

Are you satisfied with where you are in life? Are you pleased with the success you have achieved thus far? Have you realized or begun to realize your dreams? Do you understand that you are the director of your life?

Once you comprehend that you are the only one controlling your reality, you will never be the same again. You are the Vincent van Gogh of your world. Van Gogh created his life in the artistic world and drew images constructed with his wild imagination. We have been told, asked, and conditioned to be more rational than Van Gogh was. "Rationalize" (pronounced "rational lies") means to come to a sensible lie or to talk yourself into staying in your comfort zone and suppressing your imagination.

Some of the greatest inventions and the endless forms of the conveniences we use daily were created by some of the wildest imaginations ever known to humankind. Imagination, when fueled by desire, steered by faith, and continued through perseverance, is brought to life when carried by gratitude. Proof, as they say, "is in the pudding."

Look at the technological wonders that have come about just in your lifetime so far. When you begin tapping into your gifts, you begin producing satisfaction in your life in many ways that you may never have thought possible.

One of the main ingredients to satisfaction or self-fulfillment is personal management. Time spent on something you have no control over is time wasted. Many people dwell on things from their past—events that happened many years ago and cannot be changed. Some even fret over circumstances that don't directly involve them and that likely will never affect their lives in any significant way. The only way any of these things could affect them is by causing chaos and havoc through their mind-set. Looking forward to the future and putting into motion the plans to accomplish dreams and goals is a much better way to spend your time.

This personal managing has nothing to do with time management. Indeed, time can't really *be* managed. You can't make it grow, shrink, slowdown, or speed up. It just is and *IT* is all we have. Whether you are alive or dead, moving slow or fast, meditating or manifesting, time is ticking right along at its own pace. You can invest in yourself only with the time that is given to you each day. In this time, do what you can with what you have. How you use the time given to you will determine your satisfaction in life.

Another important ingredient is to learn to let go. A teacher of Wayne Dyer's put it this way: "It makes no sense to worry about things you have no control over, because there's nothing you can do about them, and why worry about things you don't control? The activity of worrying keeps you immobilized." Letting go means focusing more on yourself and the things that you have a say in and can benefit from. Then some of that satisfaction stuff will begin to take shape in your life.

When we embark on a new path, we must
first let go of that which holds us back.
—Unknown

Another helpful tactic is to lower your expectations temporarily, at least until you have a foundation and a strategy for achieving your desires. I know you've heard this before, and if you feel as most do, it will rattle you some. Think of an arrow and a target as an example. You can't expect to pick up the bow for the first time and nail the bull's-eye. That is your goal, but you understand that it happens only with plenty of practice and a strategy for how to make it all come together. Likewise, when you've set your goals, or your purpose finds you, it may not materialize immediately. The foundation lies in setting and achieving smaller goals, with the ultimate focus in mind to take you eventually to your vision.

Example

Who is Mark Victor Hansen? And why is everyone talking about him?

In the area of human potential, no one is better known and more respected than Mark Victor Hansen. He has dedicated more than twenty-five years of his life to working with organizations and people to change their vision of what is possible. His message is simple: possibilities, opportunities, and action.

As with most of us, Mark didn't always look at life the way he does now. He had to find what filled him with satisfaction. Mark was doing great in business until 1974. That year, the raw material for his business was suddenly unavailable, and he went bankrupt. How was he going to feed himself? How was he going to face this situation and the people around him? How was he going to move on from this?

This was the perfect wake-up call for him to seek out his true passion and discover his God-given talents for serving others. Mark had always wanted to be a public speaker, so he got some tapes of speakers, and then he called Bill Gove to meet with him. Bill spent an hour of his time helping Mark, and apparently, it was time well spent. Mark left that meeting so motivated and excited over his potential new career, he contacted a few other exceptional leaders in the speaking field and met with them, too. Mark was seeking something that gave him passion, something that would allow him to re-create himself and put to use the gifts he received when he was born. Since then, Mark has looked only forward, seeking out all the possibilities related to this new journey.

This has led Mark to a life that he has designed. And yes, he has run into a few challenges that most of us would call problems, but in the end, they were no match for him, because his life is fueled with the passion of knowing that he's doing what he loves to do. Even though life is seldom perfect, it is well worth living if you are the one making the choice—the choice of living a life you design and create. Mark is called the "Ambassador of Possibilities" because he finds ways for all challenges to serve him and, at the very least, teach him something new—what we call *experience*. Just by listening to Mark speak and by reading his books, you realize that no one could ever create and become all that Mark has become without first being thoroughly dissatisfied with some dimension of his life.

Satisfaction lies in the effort, not in the attainment; full effort is full victory.
—**Mahatma Gandhi**

Mark is an internationally acclaimed keynote speaker and well known to most people as coauthor of *Chicken Soup for the Soul*. As Mark Victor Hansen would say, his level of satisfaction is *MEGA*!

Experience

Let's step back to the beginning chapter, "A Story Unlike Any Other," for an example of lowering standards to reach satisfaction. I wanted to walk again, become mobile, and be more functional than just a blinking head on an uncooperative body. It began when I woke up. I couldn't do a damn thing. In fact, even the word "thing" was too deep and abstract to comprehend—just trying to get my arms around the concept made me tired. So I began by learning and understanding how to move forward from one point to another in my rehabilitation. I had made strides to move forward physically, mentally, and emotionally. If I wanted to get to point D, first I had to master points A, B, and C. If my goal was to run, I had to learn how to walk first. The times I wanted to run without mastering how to walk, I fell on my butt!

The incorrect steps I took during my recovery set me back in my rehabilitation so many times, it seems to be a common thread during the walk of progression. We run into an "uphill climb," and often we turn back or give up. Let's remember that it is the ones who fall and pick themselves up who eventually win. Do you think I should have learned how to stand before I decided to walk? In the process of learning about the human body and its potential, I had to do what I recommended in chapter 6: I had to break down my vision into smaller, achievable steps that would enable me to build a foundation. This foundation would give me the stability to move forward in any of my endeavors to become functional again. Start with simple actions to develop the skills needed for more advanced actions. Do this, and something magical happens: the advanced actions will seem simpler because those newly developed skills are at your disposal.

After all I had been through, there was only one road to follow that would give me that feeling of satisfaction. That road is to live a life of giving by using my experience of endurance, intention, faith, and mindset to guide people through their challenges into a satisfying existence. So I went on a mission to redesign myself. To this day, I am still walking the path of my choice in personal development, and I feel that I will until I have lived out my purpose and my time here.

How I experience satisfaction is probably much like the way you feel it at times. I feel satisfaction when I have given myself to helping others and I get to see them smile with joy or relief. Satisfaction is seeing their state of gratitude, seeing them walk away with some clarity for their journey. Often, it's the simplest of things during my day that make me grin like a kid on Christmas morning. It also brings satisfaction into my life when I have the opportunity to connect with someone I would like to work with, and find that they feel the same about me. Or it may come from something as simple as taking a moment to guide someone to the correct aisle in the store, and I get to see an expression of relief and gratification on their face when they find what they've been looking for. The funny part of this is, I don't work there and am only visiting, just as they are, but I passed the very thing they want just a moment ago. What a rush of good feeling can come from something so small!

What does this have to do with satisfaction? I want you to do something a few times in one day. I call it "a touch of satisfaction." Every time you go out, make sure you take a moment to pay attention to where you are and what you can do for someone else. Yes, you may have some stale times here and there, as I have. That's when I take a *step back* and look at what can I do to move forward in my life or help somebody, just to feel a touch of satisfaction in my day.

Exercise

The best thing to do here is to think about something simple that you can accomplish, knowing that you will get some satisfaction. Take one small action toward what you are passionate about: help a stranger find an address, go for coffee with a friend, do something you truly enjoy and haven't done in a while. Just do it. As you succeed with that task, take on a bit more. With each one that you accomplish, you're building up confidence and mental strength. This primes you to take on even greater tasks. Keep doing more of what brings you satisfaction. This will raise the bar each time you do.

Chapter 9   YOUR GIFT

You have a gift hidden within you that will allow you to do anything and everything you want to do, just because you choose to and because it makes you happier. The universe is abundant. It has a plenitude of opportunities and is waiting for you to embrace yours. This means there is no competition for all that you desire. Whatever your gifts, talents, and capacities are, you need to release them for your good and the good of others. Watch yourself prosper from and through them. The universe is waiting for you to step up and put your gifts and talents to work, so that it can come and play with you in fulfilling your purpose.

I want you to know that you are a Renaissance man or woman. This means that you can do as many things as you want, for the rest of your life. You have gusto for this life, and all you need do is feed it some fuel (passion) and it will fire up your opportunity for rebirth anytime you choose. As you may already have noticed, you have total control of your life and are in command of your every action and everything that you experience and feel. There are talents, gifts, and capacities within you that you have not tapped into yet and may not even know you have, and they are waiting to be freed. Think of yourself as a gift that God is working through to complete his vision and bring miraculous times and events to you and others. You just need to declare what you want. Declare it, and you make room for it to show up in your life. As you are calling out these bountiful gifts, keep in mind that the keys to bring them to the surface faster and have them resonating with your vision is to call on them with faith, purpose, gratitude, love, and passion.

Here are a few phrases I have used and always will. At the beginning of each, be sure to state and emphasize "I am." By placing "I am" in front of anything you state, you are owning it, declaring it as a possibility. This is tremendously powerful at any point in life, especially in the design of it. Just remember, "I am" is the opening of a declaration. So make sure you're placing it in front of something you desire, because it will come to you or become you.

Examples: I am honest. I am love. I am caring. I am abundant. I am passionate. I am purposeful.

Once you are grateful for all you have now, you will begin to receive much more in life, in every aspect and realm. Be grateful for what you want, as if you had already received it, and the most amazing actions and events will occur. The events and people you begin to attract will take your breath away. When you see how smoothly it flowed, you will find yourself asking, *Why didn't I do this or learn this before now? What held me back?* You will know the answers to these questions, too, and have them reaffirmed before you finish this book.

Accept these talents lying dormant within you, which you can begin to develop and awaken today, allowing yourself to express your life fully. Pay attention to them when they appear. They will lead you to whole realms of fulfillment.

> ***If you set goals and go after them with all the determination you can muster, your gifts will take you places that will amaze you.***
> **—Les Brown**

One of your supreme gifts is the gift of self-confidence. It is rooted in the ability that God has blessed you with to defeat any adversity that life throws at you. Your self-confidence is an inside job. It doesn't come from the outside world. It is a gift to yourself, from yourself, that allows you to tap into this power. Self-confidence is not only a gift that comes free of any charge; it is also a strength that will take you through challenges and carry you through all of life's ups and downs.

Take time to seek solitude in your day, to clear your mind and visualize your desires. The gifts you are blessed with will begin to kick into gear, and thoughts you never entertained will begin to flourish in your mind, which will bring forth a new action, and this will generate an equally grand outcome. Take control of your mental programming. Know that you are capable of manifesting every one of the visions you create.

You are limitless. "God can provide you with every blessing in abundance" (2 Corinthians 9:8). During this centering time, don't be afraid to try different ways of focusing. You may even move around to different spots or try sitting in different positions. You may find meditation a key to opening many doors. I have some friends who like being completely quiet in a serene environment. Others go for a drive in the country. Some go to a museum or the mall, a coffee shop or the library, or even the park to watch their kids or dogs play. Find your centering place. This will allow you to tap into your inner self and learn of your gifts. I have found that meditation is the best way to tap into my higher consciousness and open my mind to all that's possible.

Example

Michael Bernard Beckwith, founder of Agape International Spiritual Center in California, started his spiritual journey in the 1970s. After studying for many years, he was gifted with a vision of a transdenominational spiritual community.

Michael has tapped into the talents and gifts the Lord has blessed him with, and is making the very most of them by living out his purpose here and now. He has opened the eyes of many who are seeking clarity in their lives. As he puts it, "Your belief becomes clarity, and your clarity becomes service." Michael is the perfect example of selfless service. He has been blessed with a vision of guiding others to practice and participate consciously in our own evolution as the human race. He firmly believes that your awakening to life can affect you, your family, your associates, and the entire planet, because we all are connected.

> *We are on the planet to be and express the Divine Love*
> *of God that is alive in every fiber of our being, waiting*
> *to be released through us onto our world. Living as love*
> *is a way of life that brings heaven on earth.*
> **—Michael Bernard Beckwith**

Beckwith's work as a humanitarian and a champion of peace has gifted many with true spiritual guidance. What a fulfilling way to share the gifts he has received, by lighting the path to higher consciousness for others.

Experience

It took me hours of being in a state of utter solitude to discover my gifts, talents, blessings, or whatever you choose to call them. Now, just to be clear, we don't need complete privacy or silence to search inside ourselves for the answers we seek. The greatest gift of all this was finding my solitude in a chaotic, busy, noisy, and disruptive environment—a hospital. You don't need to take off to a serene, secluded place just to connect with your higher power and the universe. Rather, you need to find this serenity within yourself. You've had moments when you just sat and zoned out for a bit, when you got lost in a thought, and the outside world didn't even leave an impression on your mind. This is the same place you can learn to go at will.

When I was in the hospital and rehab facilities, I needed to step out for a bit, even when I couldn't even sit up. I mentally stepped out and went to a place where I could see myself doing everything that I was told I could never do. In that place in my mind, I could speak to people and share how they can win in every situation by becoming so much more as they decide to learn from all they have endured.

With these tranquil, blissful, dream-filled interludes of thought, I filled my fuel tank of desire and could then pursue the gifts within with an abundance of energy. I did it in between my two-hour rehab sessions and naps. These little spells were not long, but whenever I had a few moments for myself, I would get lost in my thoughts. Eventually, they had a cumulative effect, and I pushed beyond what anyone thought medically possible in such a short time.

> *Faith is different from proof; the latter is*
> *human, the former is a gift from God.*
> **—Blaise Pascal**

In the beginning of my healing, I was not capable of conscious thought. As I started to heal, I became aware of my thoughts and learned about my gifts and how to use them. At this point, I chose to take control of my mental programming. To tap into my powerful gifts, I needed to have intention and a strong will and to be mentally present in any situation and true to myself. I became capable of manifesting the vision our Creator blessed me with. Life was good. I still had many physical, mental, and cognitive challenges, but life was great and getting better by the moment!

I was a little at a loss when I didn't feel my God-given talents come flooding in on the first attempt. I felt as though my desire to reconnect to my inner greatness was an impossible task. But I found that as long as I stuck with it and was motivated through love, kindness, forgiveness, peace, respect, beauty, and faith, I would come away having learned something new about myself and would experience something different, new, and exciting. It took many sessions of quieting my mind and putting a thought out to the universe before I could get any connection with the spirit. I needed to step into the silence because our minds are way too busy to hear the answers of the questions we ask. Once I put myself in silence I began to be aware of my hidden talents and gifts. This unexpected, improbable world unfolding inside my head opened my eyes and gave me an entirely new perspective on who I was and who I could become. I was blessed with a vision of my gifts. I MUST make the most of them! Will you make the most of yours?

Exercise

Your gift could be something so very simple that you take it for granted. It could be something you do every day, such as communicating, mediating, caretaking, managing finances, or rebuilding car engines. Maybe you're great at teaching and love it. Your gift could be doing *anything* in any field. What brings you satisfaction? What are you passionate about? What comes natural to you? What have you always wanted to explore more deeply? Do some research on it, study it, and dream build. Create a vision board with pictures and statements of what it is you desire to become or achieve. Through this process, you will either (a) stimulate greater drive to achieve your desire or (b) realize it's not a passion of yours anymore, and become aware of what truly fuels and excites you. Imagine where you can see yourself going with this.

THERE IS GOOD
IN EVERYTHING

Chapter 10

You may ask, *How is that possible? Are you saying there is good for every bit of garbage that happens?* Yes! There is always a shiny side to the coin. We live in a dual world. Where there is a *down,* there is an *up.* When there is an *in,* there is an *out.* You get the point, right? Everything you see or experience has its opposite. Everything that has happened in our life, and all that is in this world, has more than just one perspective. There are people who always look for the worst and, therefore, manage to find the negative in every situation. And there are the others in this world who can find the positive side and the possibilities in the grimmest situation! With every obstacle in your life, you can focus on the limitations it presents, or you can see it as an opportunity for growth and find ways to benefit and grow.

> *Believe and your belief will create the fact.*
> **—William James**

In every situation, we have choices. We make thousands of choices every day. Some are vitally important, and some are of little consequence. The results are often either negative or positive—leaving you with two additional choices. The first choice: Do you see it as a good or a bad circumstance? From the answer to your first choice, you have a second choice: What are you going to do with that circumstance? How are you going to let it affect you? Is it going to hold you back, or is it going to instruct you? Will you bury your head or will you stand tall?

We can choose to look at everything we encounter throughout our day from another point of view, a different perspective or mind-set. You can find something good about it or something you have learned from it that will help you guide others on their path. As you learn your lessons, it becomes easier to go through similar experiences and help others.

This goes for every scenario you may come across in your mental, physical, spiritual, or emotional walk in this life. This also includes your family, friends, and business environment. When you feed into your will, not just to survive but to live, you will find purpose in everything.

> *You only see the objective, the obstacle must give way.*
> **—Napoleon Bonaparte**

You will begin to see that every problem has a solution that can serve you. Moreover, when you take on all challenges with a passionate intention, you are shifting from a reactive to a creative mind-set. You will know how to tap into higher levels of consciousness. This can only serve you and bring you joy. This is one of the first steps that allow you to transform your life and become the master of your emotions rather than their slave. Once you can guide and channel your emotions, life is much clearer and easier to balance.

When you get to this point and find that you can balance life's emotions and actions, your life soon begins to feel as though you are living it on purpose and by intention instead of by accident or by someone else's idea of who you should become or what you should be doing with your life.

So if you always take the time to look for the good in life, you will see it there, right in front of you—all that you are seeking and dreaming of. You just need to accept it and claim it as your own. Let's take a common example that many of us have experienced at one time or another. Often, we are looking for the worst that could happen in something we are attempting. And when things do go awry, what's our comment? We say, "I told you that would happen. I *knew* that would happen." And then, when somebody else goes out and attempts whatever it is that you tried, and succeeds, we say, "Good things always happen to her. Ah, she was lucky." But maybe, just maybe, they were looking forward to possibly achieving whatever they were attempting—"looking for the good in life"—and just happen to keep on finding it. It's weird how luck suddenly makes an appearance in front of you when you're looking for it. People like Mr. W. Mitchell learning to function again, Wayne Gretzky becoming the greatest hockey player ever, or Mother Theresa being a voice of love, peace, and possibility in places where most people with a choice would never go. Nothing happens by accident. Open your mind some, take a step out, and look at it from a different vantage point. Not only will you see the situation from another angle, but that new angle will also give you a refreshed mind-set regarding this and any other challenges.

Example

Imagine for a moment having being born without arms or legs. Okay, now imagine finding something good about it. When Nicholas Vujicic was born without arms and legs, his dad left the hospital room in shock, and his mother was so distraught, she didn't hold him until he was four months old. His family was concerned about his future. What could he possibly do for himself? Little could anyone imagine that this Nick would one day inspire and motivate people from all over the world, touching lives and leaving the impression of increase and possibility on all who could accept it.

Nick does everything he needs to do on his own. He doesn't do it the conventional way, but he found a way to overcome all the challenges of having a regular day, from brushing his teeth to getting dressed. He also learned how to type on a computer, swim, and play sports, among other things.

Nick credits his faith, family, and friends with all that he has accomplished. And he has found many people along the way who have inspired him to move forward.

Nick says, "I found the purpose of my existence, and also the purpose of my circumstance. There's a purpose for why you're in the fire." He had a vision of inspiring others and giving them hope. Nick believes that the single most effective factor in overcoming our challenges is attitude and mind-set. He invites people to see the growth opportunity in every challenge and to share it with others.

> *Our attitude can be the most powerful tool we have*
> *at our disposal, and it illustrates how the choices we*
> *make can have a profound effect on our lives and*
> *the lives of those around us.*
> **—Nicholas Vujicic**

Nick travels around the world bringing his inspirational message of hope and optimism to everyone who will listen. He is living his dream of sharing and inspiring, all because he chose to see the good in his situation and make the most of it. He is living proof that there is good to every situation!

> *As he went along, he saw a man blind from birth. His*
> *disciples asked him, "Rabbi, who sinned, this man or his*
> *parents, that he was born blind?" "Neither this man nor his*

parents sinned," said Jesus, "but this happened so that the
works of God might be displayed in him. As long as it is day,
we must do the works of him who sent me."
—John 9, 14

Experience

At times, I feel as though I am still in search of a gift that can serve more than just me. Then there are other times, when I can see sharing my journey of rebirth, of what is humanly possible, and the insight of the human potential as a gift in itself. I searched all over to see if I could create a gift that would enable me to provide service for others, and I realized after my extensive search that the gift lies within. It only needed some of my attention to ignite, stimulate, and enrich. We never need to search too far for the gift we're looking for.

God is able to provide us with every blessing in abundance.
—2 Corinthians 9, 8

You may ask what good I could possibly find in getting almost killed, losing my businesses, and enduring painful daily rehab for four years. Well, from a first look at that challenge and after all I had endured, you might say, "It's over, Daniel. There's not much you can do about it. Take it as it is and deal with it." And indeed, many people did say as much. When I finally came around and was mentally strong enough to hold a thought, I came to a very quick conclusion about where I was and why. I saw two ways to look at the situation:

- My life is over and I just have to accept it, because there's nothing I can do about it. Or . . .
- With everything that is wrong, I must find another way to look at it and see how this can serve me to serve others. There is always a lesson in every encounter in life.

So now the motorcycle was written off, I was physically beaten up, and I was unable to stay alive on my own. Physically, I had some massive injuries—heck, part of my body was paralyzed! Even though I couldn't move my left side and was told it would never work properly again—face, arm, leg, my entire left side—the shiny part of it all was that I had a deep faith in our Creator, and a passionate intention that my body would eventually work again. Other people at the hospital and rehab centers, staying on the same floor I was, were perman

ently paralyzed or had severed limbs. I would remind them to be grateful that their challenge was only as rough as it was, for they could have had it much worse in many ways. Where we were, you had only to look to find someone worse off or hear of something someone had been through that you couldn't have imagined possible. This would open people's eyes and show them that they were actually in better shape than they thought, and they would find themselves filling up with gratitude and hope.

Every day, I see things beyond anything I could imagine, because I live in the medical rehab industry. I have heard story after story, many of them horrific and tragic. Still, with everything that has happened to you, you can either feel sorry for yourself or treat what has happened as a gift. Our experiences shape us; it is our choice *how* they shape us. Everything is either an opportunity to grow or an obstacle to keep you from growing. Remember, you get to choose.

> *Life is continuous education. If you*
> *choose to learn, you will excel.*

Exercise

I know you may still be questioning this, so I will ask you to take a funky situation from the past, and another, more recent one. Take a good, long, hard look at each, and find a way for it to serve you, even if it's only that it has taught you some skill that will be of some benefit elsewhere. Every "bad" experience can always help or guide you in some way. See what you can find. What was the constructive lesson?

PART III

PREPARATION

CLAIM YOUR RIGHT

Claim your right to become all that you truly aspire to be, and live your life to your fullest potential. You will remain where you are as long as you continue to do as you have always done. Life has plenty of opportunity. There is an abundance for all to live fully. Harness the thought that you can achieve and become so much more, no matter what you have been through or will encounter. Claim your right to be happy so that you can step forward in a progressive, purposeful, and fulfilling manner. Step out of the "blind follower" mode of living your life through others' opinions, or you may find yourself not achieving many of your goals. You are so much further ahead in life than you realize if you only choose to learn and grow from all you have experienced. When you live with intention, there is a bountiful supply of energy you can harness to achieve your dreams and desires.

What you think about and speak about consistently, you will eventually bring about! Your magnificent mind goes into a process of bringing into reality what you've been thinking of. This is claiming your right by repeatedly stating all that you desire, with passion and a sure purpose behind it. Why a sure purpose? If you're asking for something you desire but have no purpose for it and can't see how this could benefit you or others, it may not come to you, or it may come to you but not in the way you had hoped, or it may pass you by at the most inconvenient, inopportune time, when you are unable to accept it.

> *Each day, improve your capacity to enjoy your life. Then*
> *you will live a life that other people want to model.*
> **—Unknown**

You deserve a constant, daily improvement to the quality of your life. Keep asking questions. There are thousands of books about personal growth, with tons of advice on how to do just that. The bottom line is, it doesn't matter what you have experienced—you can claim the right to create a better life, no matter what others say, what your upbringing was like, or what your personal challenges are! Be openly grateful for everything in your life, and know that there is a purpose to it all.

There is no need to follow the masses just to feel comfortable and be accepted. Anyone who truly listens, adapts these principles, and takes action will get results. Some results may be small yet potent, and some impressively large. It all depends on your determination, perseverance, commitment to your power of intention, and adopting this mind-set as habit. I would rather have good, creative, constructive habits than the sort that leave me empty. Which do you prefer?

Everyone who has achieved greatness in life will agree on two things:

- All that you focus on, you will bring on.
- Before you dare to achieve anything, you must claim your right to your life in this world.

This is one of the most profound steps in *The Science of Getting Rich,* by Wallace Wattles. By claiming your right, you have professed that you are worthy of all you desire. To emphasize this statement, say out loud,

"I am worthy!" Then say it once again, and add to your declarations, "I claim my right in this world."

Example

Superhero—what a story! Christopher Reeve certainly claimed his right! Of course you know him as the lead character in *Superman* since 1978. He was living proof of a man who had claimed his right! His accident on May 31, 1995, while riding in an equestrian competition, resulted in an injury to the spinal cord that left him paralyzed from the neck down.

He didn't want to live, but his wife, Dana, uttered the words that gave him the will to live: "But you're still you, and I love you." Though he faced many hardships for the rest of his life, he was determined to live as full a life as possible. Reeve found the strength to use his experience to help others after facing this devastating life blow. People came to believe he really was the true Superman. Here is a clip from his biography:

Reeve shows us the power, the possibilities and the results of a fierce and persistent commitment to growth and development. With God's help, Reeve is Superman:

- because he survived the horse riding accident and challenged himself physically during countless months of painful physical therapy,
- because he remained committed to his role as a loving husband and doting father,
- because he kept hope alive in the face of injury and paralysis that can destroy all hope in the face of having to depend on his wife and many others to feed, wash, change, move and carry him to the doctor, and
- because he came to the conclusion that God still had something for him to do.

So Christopher Reeve turned his focus away from his paralysis and began figuring out how he could live afresh. Reeve decided that a lot of people might like to hear his story. Instead of limiting the communication of his story to letters, books and videos subject to edit, Reeve chose the lecture circuit. That meant showing up in public, allowing the public to gawk at his incapacity, talking about his condition and sharing lessons learned.

Christopher Reeve certainly claimed his right to life before and after his accident. Now you can see how he, along with every other example in this book, had a predetermined mind-set and how it can make you or break you.

After his injury, Christopher Reeve traveled around the United States speaking and hosting events. He created and directed documentaries and was nominated for an Emmy Award. Christopher and Dana Reeve created a foundation that raised more than $60 million in research grants and for nonprofit organizations to improve the quality of life for people with disabilities.

If Christopher Reeve hadn't had the intention to break through this challenge and make the most of what he had after that severe injury, he wouldn't have lived as long as he did after the accident.

So… do you think Christopher Reeve claimed his right to life? Will *you* go that extra step and claim your right?

Experience

After waking from the coma, I couldn't speak. Even entertaining a thought was arduous exertion. I had no sense of hearing, and I couldn't see. When I finally began to see, I saw only shadows; then they coalesced into black-and-white images. I could feel the energies of the medical people, and I felt the vibrations of their words. I felt them say there was very little chance that I would ever do or become much more than I was at the time, and that due to my injuries, I would need to be plugged in for the rest of my life and be basically nonfunctional. These thoughts and words that I felt from the health care professionals in my room were confirmed at a later date with my family. A more predominant thought that I entertained consistently was, *I will not allow your opinions to become my reality!* They are your opinions; you keep them." That thought played over and over in my head. The moment a thought of that low vibration entered my mind, I would almost instantly nullify those energies with empowering intentions of growth, gratitude, love, peace of mind, and superabundant thoughts of the possibilities for what I *will* do.

As I was going through the daily rehab the doctors constantly asked me about my thoughts and feelings. I was encouraged to share. To be completely honest with you, I was feeling comfortable with where I was, knowing that it was only temporary. And I thought they cared, so I shared my personal vision, believing they could see my potential and feel my passion to burst through the barriers and set new standards. I found that they didn't believe that any of it was possible, just as you, too, will find that many people around you don't see or believe in your vision. I'm just giving you a heads-up that most people don't believe in much outside their own little box of what personal experience has taught them. Even then, they still second-guess and invalidate much of what they have seen or felt in this world. What I'm trying to say is that unless there is an unbreakable love and trust supporting you, you will need your passions backed up by your intentions and fueled with your mind-set. If you want to overcome everything that stands in the way of your success, and live life to your wildest expectations, this will be the only way. Oh! And, yes, remember *faith*. Your faith is the key to every single action you take. It will see you through to the end of your journey.

Then (back to my story) comes the day they need to report my progress to the insurance company. The reports said that because of my head injury, I was not completely aware of my handicaps. And I wasn't. They also said I was a dreamer and I didn't grasp my reality completely. "He has big dreams and goals that *normal* people would not dare entertain." Finally, they realized that I was anything but normal. If "normal" meant not wanting to create a better life for myself, then I certainly wasn't normal! I will move forward to achieve my dreams, and after I achieve them, I will dream some more. This is where I made a conscious choice not to allow others' opinions to become my reality! You create it as *you* see it.

I am eternally thankful that our Creator gave me strength to see beyond their small opinions and to keep expanding my dreams and visions. This was also largely supported by the teaching of experts who have endured and pressed beyond others' lack of vision—people such as Anthony Robbins, Brendon Burchard, Deepak Chopra, and Wayne W. Dyer.

We all have been around people of limited vision who did not believe in us. These people think of what *they* cannot do, and then try to pass this opinion on to us. Right or not, that's all it is: *their* opinion. I followed my own beliefs and claimed my right to walk, hear, see, and speak again, and guess what. I achieved them all!

If you would like to see what is possible when you believe passionately in yourself and have a serving purpose behind your actions, you can visit my Website at www.danielbaxspeaks.ca. My passion is creating my own business to share my story and bring a message of hope and empowerment to people like you. It doesn't matter how dire things may seem—you can always turn them around for the best if you live with purpose and give with purpose.

Exercise

Claim your right to this life and this world. When you feel you have something you should do and you feel that it's calling you, claim it! It just might be what brings you peace and fulfillment. Take that first step in bringing it to life, whatever it may be. You have read the chapters "Nothing Happens by Accident" and "Design It as You Choose It." It's time to design your life and claim it as yours. Research. Enroll. Construct. Do whatever you feel you must do. Claim it as yours. Now is the moment. Now is all we ever have. There is nothing we can do about the past, and we are busily creating the future right now. Your future is counting on you.

Chapter 12

CREATION

S o here we are now, celebrating the rebirth of your magnificent mind. We are living, breathing examples of what we can and will create when we alter our mind-set and unite our thoughts and beliefs with our actions. Thoughts lead to feelings, feelings lead to actions, actions lead to outcomes, and your outcomes create your life. Right now you are sitting on an opportunity of one of the greatest re-creations of mankind: yourself!

Just to show you what determination will create when you have your thoughts and actions running in perfect sequence or harmony, think of a time when you wanted something to happen. You talked about it, whether to yourself or to others, you dreamed about it, and you imagined it happening. You put all your attention on your goal.

- *Attention:* the act or state of applying the mind to something.

Once you placed your attention, you could visualize or imagine what you would do when you achieved it, and it felt so real, you began to take action! Whether the action was small or big, the point is, you had begun. You had intention!

- *Intention:* a determination to act in a certain way.

If you can see it in your mind, you can hold it in your hand.
—Bob Proctor

Intention is a wonderful tool of the mind. It will have you stretch toward your vision in ways you never would have imagined, until you have decided to take action. You will also begin to draw your vision and its vibrations toward you. Intention brings you both together in another dimension, at the right place and the right time. It is your choice to prepare yourself to be open and ready to accept it when it comes, or it will be like all the other things you wish or hoped for but were not prepared for and, hence, watched as they passed you by. When you focus every day on your outcome, you will be able to get each detail done with minimal effort. You will attract people, events, opportunities, or things that will help you or even do it for you, accomplishing your intentions for the day.

Be in the moment! Be here, be now, and be in touch with what you are striving for. This is immensely important, for it places you on a higher vibratory level that resonates with your focused thoughts. When you are in this higher vibratory state you will see, feel, know, and experience things that move you in ways to bring you ever closer to your outcome. It is like being in a study or mastermind group. You get in touch with a higher consciousness in another dimension, and the answers come to you as if out of nowhere. They were always there—you just tapped into the knowledge that lies within, and awoke your higher consciousness. This is often tapped into through meditation (quieting your mind), deep study, or a mastermind group.

As so often happens, when you finally achieve your desire you hear others say, "You're lucky." "The stars must be shining on you."

"Good things always happen for you." But luck has nothing to do with it. What you create in your mind and consistently talk on and think on, you eventually bring into your reality! Your mind will find ways to put you in places, in front of people, and bring possibilities to you that you never thought possible. When you believe in your imagination and your dreams with as much certainty as you believe in your next breath, you know they will be there for you. Your intention for life will come to you as surely as the air will flow into your lungs.

> *If you are capable of dreaming it, you*
> *are capable of creating it in your life.*
> **—Mark Victor Hansen**

Create a physical image in your life that resonates with your vision and passion for the rebirth of who you want to become.

Example

Not many people haven't heard of Lance Armstrong. Lance's athletic career began when he was 10 years old, cycling and competing in triathlons. By the age of 16, he was already a professional triathlete, but he decided to focus on cycling. He is well known for winning the Tour de France seven consecutive times—*after* being diagnosed with testicular cancer.

By the time Lance was diagnosed his cancer had metastasized from his testicle to his lungs and brain. In all, there were twelve golf-ball-size tumors. He was told he had a less than 20 percent chance of surviving. Using his competitive mind-set, Lance waged his battle with cancer as if it were another race to win. He began to look at it with a win-or-lose mentality. He could either win by keeping a strong focus on where he was going and where he wanted to be, or lose his life. Lance chose to win, placing himself into a high vibratory state that allowed him to heal.

What would you attempt to do if
you knew you would not fail?
—**Robert H. Schuller**

Lance was enthusiastic about his fight as he began using a new course of treatment. Eventually, he played around with the thought of racing again, though the recovery and retraining for racing was a long, hard road. Nonetheless, he trained consistently right through the chemotherapy treatments he had to endure. Lance kept his mind-set on the outcome: not only to return to racing and compete in the Tour de France, but to *win* it. He kept in his mind that nothing would beat him. With his wife's unswerving support, he fought vigorously, even bringing his bike into the bedroom and placing it at the end of his bed. This helped him return his thoughts to racing, and it placed him in a high vibrational state that helped him heal mentally and physically.

He focused daily on the goal of riding again as he re-created in his mind the vision of himself standing on the podium and having already won the race. Lance Armstrong visualized all he would do and how he would feel crossing the finish line in first place. How many races do you think he won before he ever got back on his bike? How do you think he cleared the cancer? A constructive mind-set, focused intent, and continuous, constant improvements helped him win the battle! After his return, he didn't win just once—he won the world's top cycling competition *seven years in a row,* in addition to the many other races he participated in. That's the power of using the mind-set with a passion to reach your highest potential!

The power of re-creating yourself doesn't only work if you have endured a life-altering event. It's something you can do right now with anything that may be challenging you. This could be anything that you cannot find a way through or around. It may be just refocusing on your life, where it is you would like to go, and what it is you would like to accomplish this time around. Let's take Lance, for example. Before his diagnosis, he was physically in peak shape. So what was it that he did, and how did he re-create himself? The biggest element in all his transformation was his mind-set. He transformed his mind-set so that if he failed, it would be the worst thing that could ever happen: his death. Now, I'm not saying you must always think in such stark terms of win or lose, life or death. But if you held this standard for yourself, for the things that matter most, how much more determined would you be, and what would you accomplish? Life is wrapped up in what you think on, speak on, and stay focused on.

Experience

Before the accident, I didn't even know what my life's purpose was. I had briefly thought about speaking and had joined Toastmasters, but there was no vision. I had two companies (construction and window cleaning), which I wanted to expand by opening franchises. Also, I was very fit and enjoyed the sporting life. I would work many hours a day, then come home and go for a bike ride, work out, or go on a little hike with the dogs. I always loved to be fit and find adventure in life.

I really enjoyed the construction work and the biking, but I knew there was more that I could do for myself and others. Something kept telling me I needed to give more and do more, but I ignored the "signs." I had a vision to grow my businesses, but there was still something missing in the way of a greater purpose that I could serve. I was not manifesting anything into reality, because I was not sure what it was that I wanted to do. I felt as though there was no need to change anything in my life. I was healthy, I was fit, and the businesses were doing well.

I was oblivious of the truth about where I truly was mentally and spiritually in my life. At this stage, I was still learning who I was. I was more concerned about the material world, and my relationship with the Creator was still a fairly trivial aspect of life. I cared about others, just not in the way that I do now. I was asking questions such as, *What do I do now to make more money? Where should I go from here to grow my business? What more should I be doing so I can have more?* This is where the ignorance comes into play in my life: I would ask questions of our Creator, but then I wouldn't listen when I got answers I wasn't comfortable with. What came back to me felt corny or boring or wouldn't make me immediately happy. I was too caught up in ego. I didn't value the opinions of the outer world, so I was praying and meditating, asking the universe for advice—but when it came, I still wasn't listening. I didn't understand that the answers coming through were the ones I truly needed to listen to. I just didn't think they were going to take me where I wanted to go in life at that time (even though I had no clear idea of where that was).

After the accident, it became clear to me. My purpose was and is to serve, guide, and help others in ways that enable them to learn and grow through their own experience, good or not. Having found my purpose, I make it a daily action to re-create in my mind this vision of what my purpose is, so that it becomes a reality of mine. Everywhere I go, I smile at every spirit's path I cross. Wherever I can, I lend a hand to make someone's day better. Writing this book to inspire others who have had challenges in life has been a goal of mine. Speaking engagements to teach and to guide are also on my agenda. These avenues have helped me re-create my reality and live out my purpose in this life. I feel so much more alive knowing that I have a focus and a purpose for this life. I now listen to the inner voice, and when I ask a question of the higher creative power I tend to listen. There is the odd time that I don't listen, and in those times, things don't turn out the way I thought they should. I don't ask, *Why me?* anymore. I know why.

Exercise

Think about something that you have wanted to do for a long time and that would bring you *satisfaction* but that you haven't done, because you "don't have time" or "can't afford it" or "the timing isn't right"? These are but a few of the common excuses people use to put off losing weight, quitting smoking, building/fixing the house, improving a relationship, finding a new job, learning photography, going back to school, or vacationing in Polynesia. Now is the time to begin your re-creation. Pick one of those things you have on that list, and take action

Chapter 13

PERSONAL ATTRACTION

B y the law of attraction, you attract everything in your life. The two foundational elements of attraction are your thoughts and your feelings. Even more, the words you use—particularly those you say to yourself—are creating your future this very minute. As Yvonne Oswald says, "Your self-talk produces 100 percent of your successful results." Your thoughts and feelings dictate your actions, and your actions create your life. Personal attraction is talking and thinking about something you want or desire (or *don't* want or desire) with such intensity and consistency that the universe helps you manifest it in your life. This is what you need to understand. Whatever you want to have or do, if you keep thinking on it and speaking of it all day long with passion, intent, and love, you will begin to act on whatever it is you want, and you will manifest it in your life.

You cannot manifest a new position in life, a soul mate, a job, or whatever it is you desire if you're thinking about what you *don't like* about where you are or what you have. By thinking this way, you are only creating more of what you don't like. It will show up everywhere you go: in the gas station or even at a birthday party. Do you understand what we're talking about here? Because it plays a huge role in your life. As I said before, you are the Van Gogh of your world. Begin attracting into your life and creating everything you truly want.

> *You are the master of your destiny, captain of your soul.*
> **—William Ernest Henley**

This doesn't mean that good things will just magically start to happen because you thought some good things and were positive about it all. The law is very simple. You must *take action* on those thoughts and feelings, and this will guide them into reality. When you do, you will begin to attract people, objects, situations, experiences, opportunities, health, wealth, or whatever you have been focusing on. Your results depend totally on your mind-set and on the thoughts you are constructing.

Shift your energy and focus from possible circumstances of loss and pain to a higher energy of what it is you intend to manifest in your life, and keep them there. Your thoughts and feelings attract circumstances the way nectar attracts bees. The sweeter something is, the more the bees are attracted. And the sweeter and more upbeat your thoughts are, the more you attract like-minded life and energy to you. The more intense your thoughts and actions are, the more likely you are to strike the curiosity button and draw people in like a magnet.

Anytime you find yourself thinking of what it is you don't like, or anything else in the lower realm, shift your mind back to what it is you desire, and say it aloud—loud enough that you can hear it. This will compound the effect of the desired thought in your mind. First, have the thought of it. Second, state it aloud. Third, you just heard it, so it has come into your being three times as strong as the less happy thought.

> *There has probably never been a more critical time t*
> *han right now to learn to shape your own destiny.*
> **—Bob Doyle**

If you change how you feel about things, you will change how you think about them, and so your world around you will also change. What you think about all day long, you will bring about.

Example

Bob Doyle is living his dream life because he learned how to attract to his life what he wanted. It didn't start that way, and it took him time to discover, learn, and practice the law of attraction in his personal life. He used to work for a good paycheck, not because he loved his job but because it gave him security. When he quit his job without having a backup plan, and his personal finances hit rock bottom, he made a drastic change in his life. Now, this is not something that I necessarily recommend for everyone, yet it is an example of committing yourself to something of greater purpose. Along the way, as Bob began seeking out knowledge, he found out how the law of attraction truly works and how to apply it in his personal life. Then things started to change slowly for the better. He made these changes because he decided to create his own reality. He wanted to learn about the law of attraction and teach others to use it as well.

One day during his journey, as he tried to apply it and things got worse and worse, he decided he was going to ask the universe for direction and would listen and follow his intuition without second-guessing it. Then he started to think and feel what he really wanted out of his life, and he set the intention to learn how the law of attraction really works. Then something amazing happened. Somehow, he started to receive the information he needed through unrelated situations, and as he received this information his life started to change forever. He understood how the law works, and he started to live every moment by Napoleon Hill's principles of success:

1. Like attracts like
2. Focus causes expansion
3. A pleasing personality

4. Definiteness of purpose
5. Going the extra mile
6. Mastermind alliance
7. Enthusiasm
8. Positive mental attitude
9. Self-discipline
10. Applied faith

By following these principles at all times, his life began to shift little by little. Once he had found his sense of purpose, he began to have a strong and guided focus on his intentions for life. Bob also began to attract the people, events, and things into his life that guided him in a direction that has allowed him to create the life he lives today and to do all the things he has done.

Experience

Before my accident, I was already living the law of attraction. I was a go-getter. My businesses took off because I was focused on getting work using my training and skills in doing for others what they could not do for themselves. I would be driving down the road, and when I saw a need (a house or property to be fixed or windows to be cleaned), I would say to myself, *they need some work done, and by the end of the week I will be doing the work they need done.* I would then take action and approach the person in charge or the owner of the property, talk about their needs and how I could meet those needs, and get the job! The only difference was that I didn't know I was using the law of attraction until *The Secret* came out and I began to read more on Earl Nightingale and Wayne Dyer's work.

I was in rehabilitation when the movie *The Secret* hit the screen. One of my therapists told me that every time he watched it, he would think of me. He gave me a copy and told me I needed to see it. So I watched it—over and over and over again! It made me realize I was already working with the law. Watching the movie only gave me greater clarity on the benefits of this law and what you can accomplish when you apply it with conviction.

Believe me when I say that I had to *work* at this to make it happen. I needed to understand what I was doing right and what I was doing that completely contradicted the flow I wanted to move in. I could not just wish it into my life; I had to take action—purposeful and focused action. For example, the only reason I could meet and spend some time with Anthony Robbins, Bob Proctor, and Marc Victor Hansen was because I bought tickets to see them. They did not come to me; I went to them. They came into my life because I got into their environment and because of what I said, how I said it, and to whom I said it. In other words, if I hadn't placed myself there and spoken with the people who connected me with them, it wouldn't have happened. It may cost you some money and time to put yourself into these positions, but what you get in return will be worth tenfold what you put out when you make your intentions clear.

> *Whatever you think you can do or believe you can do,*
> *begin it. Action has magic, grace and power in it.*
> **—Johann Wolfgang von Goethe**

The same thing applied to my rehabilitation. It started with the therapists working with me until I could eventually smile with both sides of my face. I worked hard at it, and once I did smile fully they were so proud to see what I had accomplished, it inspired me to do more. Once I did more it inspired them to work more with me. It got to a point where they knew I was going to walk and talk whether they helped me or not. I made a deal with the therapists that I would not try to walk on my own but would work with them to avoid additional injuries. What actually happened was the law of attraction. I thought about it and talked about it so much, it actually brought the therapists into my life to help me realize many of my dreams and desires of becoming mobile and functional again. I created such a passion and conviction within myself that I knew nothing was going to stop me from achieving it. The therapists saw this, and they were inspired to do more with me, pushing me to the reasonable limit and permitting me to push beyond with their support.

Being aligned with the laws of the universe has led me to places and brought people into my life most people only dream of. Where I have gone, whom I have met, and what I am doing to this day, I owe to the spirit. Listening to the inner voice has kept me connected to the higher power in this universe.

I take time daily to meditate and just be silent. It is when I am silent that I can clear my mind of the chaos around me and connect with my spirit and our Creator to pose my questions. Meditating opens me up, which allows our Creator to work through me. It brings me much closer to God than when I have my mind running like a herd of cats, in every direction at once. Having a close relationship with God gives me a stronger awareness of his presence and of the infinite wealth and abundance he is waiting to give me. When I return to a conscious state I am calm and can see clearly the paths I need to follow.

Exercise

Visualize all that you desire to achieve. Allow the visions and feelings of your intention to flow through you completely. Write out your thoughts and your feelings. Once you begin this seeking process all sorts of serendipitous things will begin to happen. You'll connect with people you never thought you would see, or do things that you thought were out of your hands. The laws of the universe have brought them into your life. Enjoy and celebrate your success.

FOCUSED THOUGHTS

Chapter 14

We all have been created equal. No one is born with more value than another. The difference between someone who succeeds and someone who doesn't is that some choose to use the gift of thought and energy that our Creator has given us all. People who succeed put much more focus on their desires, dreams, and goals. As we know, once their thoughts went out into the universe, they put themselves into a position of positive attraction to bring it all into their reality, as Bob Doyle did. This is done by a conscious and consistent focus. This doesn't mean you must focus on the thing you desire EVERY second. What it does mean is that your predominating thoughts should be of this nature. Some opportunities have appeared to you at times in your life, but because you may not have been focused on your intention, you didn't recognize those possibilities, and you missed them.

Where there is no vision, the people perish.
—Proverbs 29, 18

Once you start using the law of attraction to your benefit through conscious and consistent focus, all will come to you in such a powerful way, it may catch you a little off guard until you get used to the speed of the universe. Most brush it off as fate, coincidence, or luck at first, and never pay any attention to it. This is when you need to pay attention and take note of what your last action or thoughts were that may have allowed this to happen. You will realize that you had everything to do with making it happen. Soon you'll get accustomed to the outcomes of your thoughts; you will strive and yearn to feel this joy daily: giving, helping, and benefiting yourself and others along your path. The power and focus of your thoughts will be amplified when backed by the thought of giving. Hold a mental image of your passion, dreams, or goal with absolute certainty that you will receive it. Your life is ever expanding with possibility. When you have infinite patience, everything you desire shows up immediately. Speak of it or think of it only with the passion with which you aspire to it.

In a way, you can think of yourself as a giant electromagnet from a scrap yard. When turned on, it attracts all the metal in its field. When your energy is diverted or unfocused it's like having that giant magnet turned off, and it releases the metal—drops it like a hot potato. Well, to get in your face just a bit, you do the same thing. That's what energy does.

A traffic ticket, a soul mate, getting fired, getting promoted—you brought it all into your life. I can feel your thoughts from here. You're thinking, *sure Daniel, if you say so—but I don't think so. Why would I call for anything I don't like or don't want! Good things, yes; painful things, no thanks.* But sit back, take a moment, and visualize what you were just thinking before the last memorable event, when you received something or something was taken, or even when you stubbed your toe. I'll bet you that when you received something good, it was a good energy (a high-vibration frequency) you were sending out; when the unpleasant thing came your way, you were putting out a negative energy (a low-vibration frequency). Deep down inside you, what were you expecting?

As the energetic magnet you are, you either attract or repel the goodness that you deserve in life. Again, be sure to think and speak of whatever you desire, with an attitude of certainty that it is arriving. Then mentally and emotionally claim it as yours, even before it appears in the material world. See it, feel it, and imagine it! Tap into that wild imagination of yours. Begin to picture what it is that you feel deep inside: the desire for a purposeful life. Focus on what you don't have, or focus on what you want—either way, you'll always get more of what you're focused on. Pay attention to the wonders in life and you will live in wonder. Mentally and emotionally create it. When you believe in it, that's when you will achieve it.

Remember, your first step is to believe in your thoughts. Your belief and your faith in what you have imagined must be so strong that it will become true or come to you. If you are determined, you will *go that extra mile* to bring your thoughts to life.

> **Optimism creates energy and is contagious.**
> **—Denis Waitley**

Example

If you've seen *The Secret,* you know who Morris Goodman is. He's "the miracle man." One day, Morris took his airplane out for a flight, and as he was landing, the plane got caught in power lines and crashed. Morris made it to the hospital alive, but his life was changed forever. He was completely paralyzed; he could only blink his eyes. Morris's neck was fractured in two places, his diaphragm was not working, so he couldn't breathe on his own, his swallowing reflex was gone, and nothing—no food or drink—would go down his throat. On top of that, his voice box was so damaged, he couldn't talk. His injuries were so severe, doctors did not expect him to survive.

But Morris didn't give up. He decided to listen to the inner voice that told him, *You can make it!* It took him a long time, and he had to withstand the physical pain from each effort, but he was determined and focused on recovering his body's functionality. The first thing he decided to do was to breathe on his own. He consciously made the effort with his muscles to breathe, and he repeated it countless times until his body started to breathe partially on its own. Morris kept working out his muscles until he was taken off the ventilator. He imagined himself having a normal life and walking out of the hospital. The only thing he had to work with in the entire hospital was his mind, so he made a choice of what to focus on.

> *Deliberately seek the company of people who influence*
> *you to think and act on building the life you desire.*
> **—Napoleon Hill**

Morris Goodman's road to recovery was a Herculean task. Eight months after the crash, he walked out of the hospital, but it took him about five years to regain his life. It is his focused thought on his passion to function fully once again that has gotten him this far in recovery and continues to drive him forward to excel in his life.

Experience

Focused thought has brought to me—and still brings—many things in my new life: new and exciting journeys, open doors, and opportunities to meet people who can guide, assist, and teach me. This has given me opportunities to do things, and it has taken me to places that most people only dream of or read about.

While the healing and movement was beginning to manifest in my body, it required a consistent focus on feeling and moving my left side, from my eyebrow to my toe, and teaching myself to breathe again on my own. I would focus on sending energy to my limbs and imagined having feeling and functional, smooth movement. A huge part of the focused intent was on healing my brain, memory, and communication skills. I figured that if I learned how to communicate to myself, and my spirit understood what I was mumbling to it, I would have a chance of connecting with another life form. It worked! Most animals understood me clearly, and dogs understood me really well! I'm still working on the humans—they're the toughest nuts to crack.

I would imagine that I felt or had sensation on my left side, so often and so intensely that when that day came and I actually felt some sensation, I couldn't be sure whether it was real or only my focused thought or imagination. I could get focus my thoughts so intently and have them take up my every waking moment because, at that time in my life, I had nothing else to think about. As I said earlier, the doctor came in and said I would probably never walk, talk, eat solid food, or move my left side. And if I did, it would be so minimal it would hardly be recognizable. It was at that moment that I focused intent on my body and mind to feel the healing energy that would allow my body to move, feel again, and function properly. This was the shift in my new life that gave me control over my possibilities and let me create my life as I imagined it becoming.

> ***Life's challenges are not supposed to paralyze you;***
> ***they're supposed to help you discover who you are.***

That was their picture of how they saw me, but it didn't matter what they saw. What was most important was how I saw myself and what I thought. They said, "*It won't happen,*" and I heard "*It could happen.*" They said "*never,*" and I heard "*now.*" They said "*impossible,*" and I heard "*Prove me wrong.*" This goes back to defining your mind-set, since that is the one thing you have full control over. It defines your purpose and your possibilities. Your mind-set allows you to design yourself and become much more than you ever were before or have ever imagined becoming. For it is in growth, over time, that we surpass our old expectations, creating our history and designing our future.

So how did I put this to work in my life, and what benefit did it bring? I'll give you two examples of what a focused thought can do for you:

I realized that when I focused on something with a consistent effort, strong intensity, an abundance of energy, and infinite patience it would always come to me. So I focused on my left foot—actually, it was my left big toe—for all my feeling and movement began on my left side. I had the full intention of having the neural pathways reconnect and build a new path to my brain so that I could regain full use and feeling of my body. I concentrated on it for as long as I could hold a thought. I did this over and over and over, with greater intensity each time, until I saw my big toe move. Once I had it moving, I placed more energy into my focus and went for the other toes, then my foot, and as we all know, "The toe bone's connected to the foot bone; the foot bone's connected to the ankle bone; the ankle bone's connected to the leg bone; now, shake dem skeleton bones!" You know how the song goes. Soon it was "left, right, left," and I am walking again—and by the time you read this I will be running.

As Mr. Goodman did, I focused on my breathing capacity, for I knew it would not be easy to do any physical activity while carting around an oxygen tank. Biking or hiking would be a definite challenge. I practiced holding my breath. The first time, it was only a few seconds. Then I could do it for longer and longer. I would pinch the cord of the oxygen line and hold my breath as long as I could, and then take deep breaths to see if I could breathe on my own. **(I do *not* recommend trying this if you must use an oxygen tank!)** When I had to breathe afterward, it forced my diaphragm to retrain itself to make the motions it was supposed to make so that I could live, and it would bring a fresh supply of air into my lungs. As time went on, I would pinch the oxygen hose longer and longer until I learned to take air on my own, completely unassisted. Then it came to a point where they took my tubes out and let me roam freely and get my air through the breathing system our Creator blessed us with. From here, I was one challenge closer to being able to *live* life and not just exist in it anymore. Neither Morris Goodman nor I would have pulled through if we hadn't refused to accept the possibility of failure or death and had not exercised our focused intent.

We developed an entirely new mind-set of what was possible and who we would become in this life.

> *Discovery consists of seeing what everybody has*
> *seen and thinking what nobody else has thought.*
> **—Jonathan Swift**

Exercise

Visualize your goal, and focus your mind-set on what you need to do and how it can be done. If you have heard unsupportive comments about it, let those thoughts go. Focus entirely on how you are going to accomplish it. Research how you can do it. Ask people who have done it or something similar. Write down a task list. Make sure each task is specific and simplified—a lot of people tend to write down tasks that are too broad and general. After you have your list, start working immediately on each task until you accomplish it.

Chapter 15

PROMOTION

As we look at any great leader, we see them promoting others and themselves. To do this, they must have confidence and security in themselves before they can promote others with such assurance.

From what I have seen and researched, anyone who has achieved greatness in life has stepped far beyond the solo, competitive *me* to have an "I" mind-set. They walk and talk at a higher vibration, entertaining only empowering thoughts. A creative, giving, and joyful mind and an understanding of the universal abundance are only some of the qualities that make up the millionaire mind-set and a million-dollar mind.

Promote inspiration in yourself by reading books, magazines, or papers on self-development or on something else you aspire to. Begin doing things that create inspiration and growth in your life. When you get enough inspiration you will be willing to overcome and push through all that is holding you back from accomplishing great things in this life. Inspiration will give you the power and energy to accomplish so much more. You will begin to see the greatness in others and will get a thrill through promoting their talents. What you'll notice is that you begin to talk less and listen more intently to find a talent or strength that you can pick up on and ask them about. By doing this, you'll gain insights into their abilities and, perhaps, discover ways that you can promote them.

> *Satisfaction lies in the effort, not in the*
> *attainment. Full effort is full victory.*
> **—Mahatma Gandhi**

Say the person you're talking to is looking for a job or a new line of work. You now have some insight into their abilities and can keep an eye and ear open for them. Or maybe they are new in the area and like to play fast-pitch softball, and you just happen to know of someone looking to start a team.

What we learn and know is this: when we set a goal—and set it with passion, intention, and purpose—it will materialize with time and effort. As we begin to live it vividly, as though it had already happened, it will inspire the momentum to begin. The trick that many miss is, that you cannot fake your excitement. People sense when you have hidden thoughts or are putting up a facade that you're happy and your belief is strong. They may not know exactly what's going on, but they will intuitively know there is something amiss. You have to believe in yourself and your goals. It's crucial to believe in yourself even when no one else does. It isn't until later, as it all begins to turn out well, that others will come around and say, "I knew you could do it!" The amazing effect of this momentum is that it places us in a magnetic field that attracts like-minded and action-oriented people. In turn, this creates a promotional nature within us, and an amazing network of people around us. These people show up only because you have placed yourself out where you can be seen and heard.

There is no such thing as a self-made man. You
will reach your goals with the help of other people.
—George Shinn

This is very similar to having a child. The more you do for them and the more happiness and excitement you bring into their lives, the more you get to watch them express their happiness, and this will inspire you to do more. Let me tell you of a personal experience that probably has a familiar ring for you: When my dad tickled me, it made me laugh more and more, and in hearing my laughter and glee, he would keep tickling me until my face and tummy hurt. This is an extreme example, though it plays out the same in all realms of life. Dad did it because he was bringing me joy. This, in turn, gave him joy, and in the process he promoted happiness all around the house. Then my brothers and mother would begin to laugh and join in the tickle game. Be warned, though: it's infectious!

We connect with others the way we do, to raise them and ourselves to a state of joy. It brings you tremendous joy knowing that you just gave to someone. This places you in a higher frequency, from which you can continuously give and enrich all paths you cross. As the Bible says, "Give and it will be given to you" (Luke 6, 38). This is totally awesome! Everything you give comes back to you multiplied, in an endless variety of ways, as long as it was given from love, gratitude, or any other powerful creative emotion. The key point to all this is to promote others, expecting and wanting nothing in return, and you will promote yourself, because others will promote you!

Example

Oprah Winfrey didn't just happen to stumble onto her success. She was diligent and purposeful in her actions and in what she intended. She placed herself in the right places and then began promoting herself by doing and living her word. She used the media as a tool, along with her will and her drive to raise other people's spirits.

Oprah has created a connection with people around the world by promoting, enlightening, uplifting, and supporting all kinds of people throughout her broadcasting career. Her drive to find out more and learn the truth has motivated her to look even deeper into situations. While doing this, she has always promoted someone along the way.

Oprah didn't become so well known around the world just by focusing on herself and how far she could get in life on her own. She paid attention to the dreams and desires of others, by helping them follow through with their passions and reach for their goals and by helping them overcome their challenges. If you do things of this nature openly and naturally, it can only reflect your true nature. You can perceive and know people's true nature by their actions. Action speaks a thousand words.

If you have seen Oprah's show or read her magazine, then you know that she is always promoting someone or something she believes in. When serving others, our goal must be to help them accomplish their purpose, enriching them along the way. The last thing that should be on our mind is, *How can I take advantage of this?* Walking her talk and talking her walk throughout her life has led Oprah to where she is today: one of the richest (in all aspects of life) and best-known people in the media, with an impressive career of service through promoting another's soul. When you guide, uplift, support, and promote someone else in a loving and empowering form you are practicing the best form of self-promotion you can possibly do.

> *The joy one gets while promoting*
> *another's joy is incomparable.*
> **—Sri Sathya Sai Baba**

When you go out of your way to seek the truth of someone's greatness and share it with others, they can see only the greatness in you. From what I have learned and seen, this is one of the sure ways to show character and to promote yourself without having to go around telling everyone how good you are and what you can do. Stay humble.

It is a very natural and spiritual way of lifting yourself up as you lift up another. When you speak with truth and are honestly open with the intention to uplift and enrich another, you can only promote yourself to the world as a soul other people can trust, respect, and long to follow and learn from. This is what Oprah has done.

Experience

You don't have to give something tangible. Often something intangible is more meaningful. It's heartfelt and thoughtful, and it leaves a greater impression on the receiver. Kind words and actions will take you leaps and bounds further than a physical gift of thanks, pretty much every time.

I was always smiling and had a warm, exciting, and welcoming nature. Five years later, not much has changed. Giving began as an act transformed by repetition into a habit. Giving is a very powerful action, and compounded when given through gratitude and love. Gratitude and giving are in complete, harmonious alignment with each other, and they become an extremely powerful act when unified. How did I put them to use in promoting others? As my family told me, whether I was with them, the medical staff, or anyone who came to visit, I was as giving as one could be in such an incapacitated state. All I could give at the time was a half-crooked smile and a childlike, goofy sense of humor, along with copious amounts of gratitude, joy, and love.

What I had experienced—and still do to this day—was tremendous warmth and support. The medical professionals and my family made sure I was always comfortable and gave me the best care they could provide. As I regained consciousness, I was often in a state of joy, gratitude, love, and possibility. Not to say that I wasn't an ass at times—I'm certain I was. But what I found was that my being in such a creative, receptive mode promoted them to do much more than they otherwise might.

Let's step back to before that life-changing motorcycle ride and look at how promotion worked in my life to turn my passion for building and designing into creating my companies. It was before my rebirth that I began to learn about promotion by showing love and gratitude and trying to help out in any possible way. I began to do things for others when I knew they wanted or needed something, as long as I knew for sure I had the skills to do it. If not, I would seek out information on people who did, and make some calls in their behalf. I did it because I could and out of good intentions. In doing this in my businesses and throughout my day, it all came back tenfold. I never needed to promote my businesses or myself outside of supporting and giving from a loving nature. People hired my services or asked for help because they knew of me and knew of my nature and energy, even before I met them personally, through the spoken word of others sharing their experience of who I was and what I did.

This is an energy that vibrates at a very similar level to what Oprah does (though not on nearly so grand a scale). The public got to know Oprah, and she only ever needed to be her true, trustworthy self. That was promotion enough. Everyone who knew of her talked about her, and if you didn't know of her, you wanted to. For me as for Oprah, promoting others was very fitting with the way we both desired to be recognized, and it fit right in with our intention to make a difference in someone else's life.

When I was in the medical facilities I would try to help anyone I could by helping to guide them through their challenges. Sometimes I helped them; other times it didn't work out for them, but they would keep coming back, so I must have been doing something right. Over time, more people would gravitate toward me. I found myself doing "sessions" with groups of people on appreciating and promoting the kindness of the staff and other survivors, and how it comes back to you right away when you do it from a state of gratitude and love. This is what I wanted to be known for this time around: inspiring and guiding people with love and forgiveness so they can learn how to overcome the hardships of life while finding a higher awareness in themselves and awakening their higher consciousness.

> *Appreciation is a wonderful thing: it makes*
> *what is excellent in others belong to us as well.*
> **—Voltaire**

Self-promotion is exciting when you do it in such a way that you end up enriching someone else's life along the way. It is a very natural and spiritual way of lifting yourself up as you lift another. When you speak with truth and are honestly open with the intention to uplift and enrich people around you, you can only promote yourself to the world as a soul other people can trust, respect, and will long to follow and learn from.

Exercise

Whether you're introverted or extroverted, it's better to talk less and do more. If you wish to let people know what you can do for them, these are the steps I recommend taking:

1. You know you can do certain things and do them well. When you see someone who needs something done that you are good at, offer your assistance with no expectation of reward. It's important to give to those around you—just remember always to keep your own life in balance.
2. If there is something a friend, family member, client, neighbor, or coworker needs and you know you can do it without disturbing them, take some initiative and do it for them. For example, it may be something around the property, around the office, or at the club. Whatever it is, just do it, as long as you aren't intruding.
3. If you know of someone who has done something well, let them know you saw what they did, and compliment them.

Don't offer any suggestions on how they could do it better, unless they ask you. Be grateful for their thoughtful action. They may have put themselves out to do this, or it may be their first time. This will promote your ability, kindness, and love for life far greater than your telling them about your skills or what you can do.

Chapter 16

GRATITUDE

The whole process of mental adjustment and attunement can be summed up in one word: gratitude. Position yourself in a state of deep, profound gratitude. As good things come your way, you need to put your thoughts on being grateful for all you are and for every circumstance you get to learn from.

Gratitude is one of the most powerful emotions you can exercise to bring what you want into your life. Gratitude will attract what you need or want, in abundance. There is always some good to come of gratitude. There is ALWAYS the "shiny side to the coin." Speak and feel gratitude constantly throughout your daily walk. You will transform your energy frequency into one of the most powerful attractions that exist in this world. You will come so much closer to achieving your goals because you will be in passionate harmony with your dreams and desires. The exercise of gratitude will never fail to strengthen your faith and renew your purpose in life.

Hold in your mind constantly a vision of the way you want to be, where you want to go, and whom you desire to become. Envision it only in the desired state, and if you begin to see conflict or picture failure, don't entertain it. Bring your mind back to envision whatever it is that you desire, in complete detail. Imagine what you will feel like emotionally, the people you will connect with, and the experience of living it out daily. Then live out your every day with the feeling of gratitude, and have faith that all you think about you will *bring* about. Start creating it right now. Don't wait for it to come to you. You must take action on your thoughts this moment. Begin before you finish reading this chapter. Provide for the reception of all things you desire as they come to you. Exercise the will to give and the gratitude of receiving.

We all can benefit from this power. When we harness gratitude with love and use it unselfishly, it generates a force of good that cannot be bartered with. Open yourself up, pay attention, and learn that when you induce this power you have the ability to overcome anything. You will feel, throughout your being, enrichment that no material item can ever provide.

> *It takes only a single thought to move the world.*
> **—Napoleon Hill**

When you are going through times of lower vibration or when business may not be great, exercise this law of gratitude to the fullest. Remember, you must do it out of love and faith. If not, you will be playing with a lower energy, and others—and the universe itself—will see through your false front and lead you further away from what you desire. On the other hand, when you live in the higher vibrations of energy you will leave an impression of increase on all the paths you cross. Your passion for this life, and devotion to it, will shine through, and this places you in a harmonious relationship with the good in everything. Things, people, and events you desire will surface. Live and express honest, loving gratitude in all you do.

Without gratitude, you will experience dissatisfaction with most things as they are. Have the courage to follow your convictions, believe in yourself, and keep your focus, not on the possibility of failure but on the goal. Joy, fulfillment, and a state of peace are only part of the abundance of good emotions you will get to experience. The fun part is, you will be enriched every moment that you experience thankfulness and become a greater positive influence on your community and family. Live it, love it, and rejoice in life.

Live gratefully! Experience the harmonious flow and power of gratitude.

Example

Dr. Wayne Dyer is an author, speaker, therapist, and teacher of higher consciousness. He has published more than ten self-help books that have gone on to become best-sellers, influencing many thousands with his messages on motivation, spirituality, living fully, and creating abundance in life.

Dr. Dyer spent his early life in foster homes and orphanages, and later on, as a young adult, he served four years in the Navy and studied educational counseling at Wayne State University. He started off his career by teaching students from high school to postgraduate. Despite his challenging childhood, Dr. Dyer decided to learn from all he had journeyed through and from all the obstacles along the way in making his life a life of his choice. He knows that thoughts create things, for this is what he teaches, so we can learn how to do the same and make our dreams and passions come true.

Wayne Dyer lives a life of higher consciousness. He is always looking to find time when he can be in a space of gratitude, even if it's at a stoplight. Wherever we can find even a few moments, we have an opportunity to reflect and be grateful for everything we have in life. In Dr. Dyer's experience, any time you can take to feel grateful is time well spent, and it can only enlighten you more. From his observations, most people who are at the top of their fields have the attitude of gratitude and "radical humility." Here's how he puts it:

> *After all, when so many high achievers reach for their dreams and desires or the championship trophy, they say, "First I'd like to thank God." It's almost as if they can't help themselves—they're so grateful for their accomplishments. They can feel that there's a force in the universe way bigger than they are. This force allows them to accomplish feats beyond their personal best. When we adopt this kind of an attitude, we'll inspire others to do the same. If we practice gratitude as opposed to maintaining an attitude of entitlement, we'll automatically extend inspiration wherever we go. Being grateful helps remove the influence of the ego, which leads us to thinking that we're better than everyone else.*

Dr. Dyer sets an example of gratitude for all of us. He starts every day by expressing gratitude in front of a mirror, where he repeats these words: *"Thank you, God, for this life, for my body, for my family and loved ones, for this day, and for the opportunity to be of service. Thank you, thank you, thank you!"* Being in the vibration of gratitude sends a message to everyone and everything around us that we are aware and connected to something bigger than ourselves.

> ***I express gratitude for all the good in my life. Each day brings wonderful new surprises. The more grateful I am for the wealth and abundance in my life, the more reasons I find to be grateful.***
> **—Dr. Wayne Dyer**

Experience

Well, you know part of my story and what I have been through since the rebirth. I am so very grateful for having gone through all that chaos. Gratitude is a phenomenal service that brings abundance to your world in the most profound ways, at such opportune times. You may be thinking, *Daniel, how on earth could you possibly feel grateful after all you've been through?*

There are multiple reasons for feeling so much gratitude in my life today. It has slowed me down a lot. I was living a lifestyle in which I pushed myself to the limit in everything I did. I would often come home injured. As I've told you, I didn't take care of the vessel I lived in. I figured it was indestructible, so I was reckless with it. I was also very reckless behind the wheel of a car, behind the handlebars on a bike, and with anything else I got my hands on. If I had continued, I would have killed more than just myself, and that would be unbearably painful, knowing that my carelessness had caused hurt to another person or family.

> *Gratitude is not only the greatest of*
> *virtues, but the parent of all the others.*
> **—Cicero**

Where does the feeling of gratitude come into play during my life today? I am supremely grateful that I endured this challenge, for it has slowed me down and blessed me with the awareness of safety—for myself, yes, but primarily for others. I now have a strong respect, empathy, and understanding of those who have endured any sort of trauma, and this has blessed me with a passion in creating programs and events that will guide and allow anyone who intends to experience a higher level of consciousness. This is one way to provide service to people that will allow them to heal faster and more smoothly. My experience has blessed me with a greater purpose of service and support, which I wouldn't have had otherwise. I now have the gift of knowing and feeling that there is always something to be grateful for.

I do my best to give unconditionally, with purpose and love, expecting nothing in return. I do this just because I want to and because

I can, for I know that expecting nothing in return opens the floodgates, and something always comes back at the most opportune time. It's something like knowing I will be taken care of because I take care of others. When and how, only God knows—I simply have the certainty that it will be. The amazing part of living in this higher awareness and higher energy is that if you have infinite patience, you will always receive something at the most opportune time, and it often comes from a completely unrelated source. It always comes back in expanded increments, as long as I am continuously expressing my appreciation for life through all I do.

What I have learned over life and from my studies of some great people is that they are grateful for all they have achieved, where they have been, and whom they have had the opportunity to meet. They aren't just grateful once; it is an ongoing feeling they entertain regularly. I do believe they, as any of us, have days of not feeling grateful for their life or who is in it, but they don't stay there. It's a temporary state, and they make sure they leave it behind as soon as possible. The key is to realize right away where you are mentally and emotionally, and then move back into the higher vibration again and continue to experience the feeling of gratitude for all you *do* have.

For the time I was in the hospital, I showed my gratitude daily to everyone I encountered. I was grateful just for the opportunity to feel life again. I have found that when I am living life through the eyes of gratitude it keeps me in harmony with my desires in life. This attitude places me in a higher consciousness, where I attract creative energy, and then good things begin to come my way. I am grateful for all that happens. I can only learn and grow.

Exercise

Show your appreciation and gratitude to everybody when you get a feeling to do it. Follow that inner voice, and when someone does something for you, directly or indirectly, be grateful to him or her and for his or her actions. Don't overdo it, either. A simple thank-you to let them know you appreciate their kindness should be enough for now. Promote them to others and say how their kindness made you feel. Watch how far a little gratitude will take you.

Chapter 17

MOVE FROM COMPETITIVE TO CREATIVE

As you expand your awareness, you will feel yourself shift from being a competitor to being a creator, and you will begin to notice the tremendous power you have within you. Once you realize your God-given gift, you will not want to compete with another being. The moment you realize you have this power within you, you move to an entirely new level in life, one where your creative mind has absolutely no limitations. There is a plenitude of energy, opportunities, and ways for you to create greater outcomes in your life.

> *All that you desire or seek in this life is out*
> *there in this universe, and it does desire and*
> *seek you in return with equal intensity.*
> **—Bob Proctor**

When you live in a competitive mind-set, competing with others to win and to gain recognition, pride, or superiority, if you don't win that immediate challenge, you still have won if you choose to learn from it in some dimension. You will go back to what you started with, or maybe a little less, because you are going to spend your energy and time fighting for first place. But in the creative mind-set, if you don't win the game, you have still won the battle. When you are in a creative mind-set you can always find a way to learn something mentally, physically, or spiritually from what you have been through. As you do, you will find a way to triumph through your challenges, so you will come out a winner in every scenario. Having a creative mind-set will allow you to cooperate with others and join efforts in achieving greater goals.

You will learn that through living a life in a low vibration, being destructive and competitive, you will diminish or destroy your life and other lives during your walk through this life. But a high-vibration, creative mind-set sets up an energy, an intention, that is enriching and constructive.

There is one thing I've learned for sure: even though positive thinking and optimism is not enough to create a successful life, it is definitely the beginning. Thinking and feeling in a grateful and optimistic attitude is more than a good beginning—it's a solid foundation for your mental actions in generating a creative dynamic to last you a lifetime.

Some of the following supportive thoughts and actions would begin with altering your mind-set:

1. Thinking more in the way you would like your life to be, and taking some physical action.
2. Doing what you know needs to be done instead of waiting for it to be done for you.
3. Meditation: taking some time to be quiet, go into your higher consciousness, and ask for guidance.
4. Cleaning up your environment mentally and physically.
   - Start by removing disempowering items such as clothes that don't make you feel good when wearing it or looking at them.

- Disorganization clutters your home and mind. Wipe out habitual disempowering thoughts, such as looking for the worst in things, or thoughts that leave you thinking, *Why me?* or *I'm not good enough.*
- By simply tidying up your place and organizing it, you can change your world in a dramatic way. Remember that your exterior is a reflection of your interior.

Bob Proctor once told me, "Go as far as you can see. When you get there you will see how you can go further."

Example

Wallace D. Wattles is the author of *The Science of Getting Rich*. This book has everything you need to know to achieve success in every facet of your life. One of the main ideas Wattles shares is about "doing things a certain way." This "certain way" is nothing other than transforming your competitive mind-set into a creative mind-set. He explains how, most of the time, you do things dictated from your competitive mind-set. This is the mind-set that plays the CD in your brain about "scarcity of resources," "tough times," and "we are either losers or winners." It is this mind-set that keeps you mistrusting others around you and in constant competition until you are exhausted. The competitive mind-set is all about *me*. What is *my* benefit? What do *I* get? This mind-set is what keeps you looking for ways to do as little as you can for the most benefit. It is a mind-set that doesn't really care to stop for a minute and think about what happens to others around you or what their outcome was.

Wattles says that the creative mind-set is the one you were born to have. The reason for this is that it harmonizes with the universe, and as you remember, it is the universe that has all the abundance and wealth that you attract into your life. You attract wealth by playing in your mind the CD of abundance and service with purpose. The creative mind-set is the one that prompts you to help others without expecting a reward, the one that gives you solutions and lets you have win-win situations with those around you.

> *You will get all you want in life if you help*
> *enough other people get what they want.*
> —Zig Ziglar

The creative mind-set is an attitude of all the people who have achieved greatness in their lives and have shared it with others around them. Even better, the most amazing part is that you, too, have the capacity to choose this attitude and live your life from a creative mind-set. Selecting this mind-set as your daily programming will bring into your life everything you have dreamed of and even more. It is all in your attitude. You don't lose because others win. On the contrary, you win because they win with your help and support.

The creative mind-set brings wealth not only into your life and the lives of those around you, but to humanity as a whole. Just imagine a world where everyone's actions come from a creative mind-set. This planet will be a better place for us to live and to leave for those who come after us. You are changing the world by living your life with a creative mind-set.

Experience

The creative seed was planted deeply in my life through my rebirth, and it is flourishing through my developmental steps as a new man. The more I gave to the staff and patients—in uplifting compliments, assistance, and providing alternative perspectives on various situations—the more I found myself living every facet of my life fully.

Several changes began to take place in me. I felt a fulfillment in life through being creative. Habits formed with the foundation of love, honesty, and intent. I began to receive in return the energy I gave out. The least expected and the most wanted opportunities started to appear in my life. I gave myself unconditionally. I began to give time and help facilitate events that I never thought of giving my time or attention to before. As I was stepping through this new world of being creative I noticed that I began doing all sorts of things for others, just to see them smile.

The main purpose for my continuing this practice is that I love watching people blossom because of the impression my actions leave on their lives. This leaves me with an equal or maybe even greater feeling of increase in my own life.

> ### *You must never stop looking for the perfect law that sets you free.*
> ### —James 1, 25

I have heard Bob Proctor say it in a way that wraps it all up perfectly: "As you step out of the competitive mind-set and into the creative mind, as you exercise your faith and purpose on what you desire to do and give increase of life to others while making them aware of the fact that it is far greater to create than compete, they will become attracted to you and you will become rich in all ways of life."

This is my new and refreshed walk in life. I intend to live this life from the creative mind-set and focus on helping others. I have placed my focus on providing the fullest service possible for others, to the best of my ability. I love life, and it will ONLY get better from here!

Exercise

Take some time right now and review your history. Whom haven't you forgiven or apologized to? What haven't you left behind that still has you living out the regret? It's time to step into the creative and constructive energy by releasing the burdens of the pain you have endured and the pain you have inflicted. In what way can you bring enrichment and peace to another's soul? The most significant component of this exercise is that you *must* be in a constructive mind-set. If you feel any anger or pain, you won't be able to move forward until you realize you are living in a cycle that repeats itself. Letting go is easier than you think. Do what you must to let go of all those emotions and thoughts that are not bringing happiness to your life. You can double your energy by using it in a constructive way.

Chapter 18

USE OF THE WILL

The role of the will in getting the most out of your life is to keep you thinking and doing all those things that will keep you on a course of achieving. Use the will to keep yourself thinking and acting in "a certain way." When you find your mind wandering from focusing on what you want, use *willpower* to bring it back to your purpose.

It is crucially important that you pay attention to your conscious thoughts so that you don't spend time worrying, doubting, or concentrating on the unimportant, negative "stuff." The simplest way you can pay attention to your thoughts is by using your willpower to keep your mind focused on your intentions and dreams. This will keep you flowing in the right direction so that you begin to accomplish your intentions and fulfill your purpose in this life.

Your will is one of the key elements in all that you achieve. Spend your time constructively believing that your desires will come to pass, and summon your will. Together, your will and concentration are a strong key to your success. When you unite your will and concentration, you will have brought together two of the most powerful faculties you possess, and you will have released an unfathomable power for accomplishment.

You have will and purpose in life. Feed it. Spread your wings!

People do not lack strength; they lack will.
—**Victor Hugo**

If you're thinking of an outcome merely by hoping or wishing that it might (if you're lucky) come waltzing into your life, you're giving it a very loose chance of being created. There is a definite way that all we desire will come to pass, and that is by *will*. Will is the captain of the ship of success. It gives orders to the rest of your faculties on how they need to perform and whom you must connect with to make all that you want come to fruition

All that you need and could ever want is already out there. There is an endless supply in the universe of everything we desire. As Wallace D. Wattles says in *The Science of Getting Rich,* "With thought, all is brought to you; with action, you receive it." Use your mind to form a clear mental image of what you want, and use your will to make sure that you hold on to that vision continuously until you embrace it. Entertain productive thoughts, and put your belief and focus on the possible into the power of the will.

Example

Tony Meléndez is a gospel composer, singer, guitarist, and author from Nicaragua. He was born without arms because of a medicine his mother took during pregnancy. Since he was young, he had to learn how to use his feet to compensate for the arms he didn't have. Born into the life of musical parents, he received a guitar from his father. Although he never truly thought he would use it to make music, he would practice six to seven hours daily, strumming the guitar with his feet until the first notes started to sound.

Tony recalls that his father used to tell him, "Tony, you have to try. You have to do it yourself." And he did. His family moved to the United States looking for better medical attention for Tony. He once had artificial arms made, but he stopped using them, because he felt that he could do much more with his feet.

When Tony played the guitar and sang for Pope John Paul II in 1987 in Los Angeles, he was sent on a mission to give hope to the world—a message that we can do so much more than we ever thought. All we need is the desire, the disposition, and the will to move forward with what we have now.

As Tony says, "We have *everything* because we are complete in God's eyes. Let go of the resentment against life, others, or yourself for not having what you want right now, or the feeling of how unfair is life."

Imagine if Tony had lived in anger and resentment because of the comments and stares he got throughout his life. Imagine if he hadn't the will to practice playing guitar so many hours. Imagine if he had given up on his talent because he didn't have arms. He would have missed the miracles he has now in his life. He would've missed playing for the pope and millions of people in forty countries around the world, doing what he loves to do. Take a quick look at the some of the significant life-altering and enriching opportunities Tony would have missed out on. Tony would have missed writing his book *A Gift of Hope*. He would have missed having a wonderful wife and children. He would have missed out on his purpose in this life.

The point here is, he is enjoying all this because he let go of the pain, self-pity, and fears to live a life of faith, love, and abundance. He has dedicated his life to inspire and bring hope to people around the world, especially youth. His message is, "Open your arms with a yes to a world that is waiting for you to make a difference in it."

We may feel incomplete or unprepared to start right at this second, but if not now, when? When are we truly going to feel we are completely ready to do what our heart desires? The moment cannot get any better than now. Now is when our heart tells us to move forward, toward our goal. The tools we need, we will receive along our journey. We will get only as far as the power of our will; it doesn't matter how much we plan or think about what we want. Without the will, there is no action. Without action, there is no achievement. The most important part of achieving is having the will to keep practicing even when we may not be entirely sure of the outcome. Always remember, one step forward is one step closer. That step means that you are already winning in your journey. As long as we have passion for what we do and we transform our will into action, we are fulfilling our mission in life and building a better world for ourselves and everyone around us.

Experience

Although I injured myself several times during my recovery, I have to say, my tenacity and my ignorance of my injuries were a gift in the beginning. As time went on, I became wiser about my physical limitations. Well, that's my opinion, anyway—many will say otherwise. Each time I hurt myself, the next day I would have no memory of what had happened or of what I could and could not do. So I often made the same mistake again, although, luckily, I did eventually begin to recall some of my limitations. Misery was knocking at my brain every time I tried to move, talk, or think about anything that required a focus longer than a few seconds. It was my faith in a higher power that kept depression at bay.

It was willpower that inspired my intention and kept me motivated to overcome all that they said was impossible and had not been achieved before—at least from their understanding. They may need to get out more!

As I listened to the guidance of our Creator, I tapped into my higher power and was led by the driving force of my will. I overcame all obstacles that were laid out in front of me, and began to regain control of my body—mentally, physically, emotionally, and spiritually.

Will gives your mind real power. Concentration, along with
your will and faith, is the key power to your success.

—**Bob Proctor**

During this walk through rehabilitation, as I became mobile I received support aids, just as Tony had been given prosthetic arms. I was given an assortment of different devices, but once I gained the initial benefit from them, I would stop using them. When the staff caught me not using them and asked why without ever truly wanting to hear my reason or intentions, they would state immediately that I needed them to do whatever it was I was doing without them. I knew I could go far with the power of the will fueled by my faith in life, the Lord, and self-determination. The use of will has been one of my greatest powers to move upward and onward to rebirth at this stage in my life. I know I am young only in years. Apparently, you can be reborn at any age, despite who you were before, what you did or didn't do, or what your accomplishments were. This isn't based on any aspect of your material world; it hinges entirety on your faith and will.

What counts most in all this has also made the biggest difference in my life. What ignited it all, made it all happen, was the combination of determination and purity of faith—that is, the power of will.

Exercise

This exercise is going to be very exciting for you. And, yes, it will entail some effort. Whatever it is that you have wanted to do, whether it's to quit a boring job and work at your passion, or to learn to run after you've been told you can never run because of blah, blah, blah, it is your *will along with concentration* that will give your mind the power to succeed. Whatever you are going to do, large or small, will yourself to do it—and then follow through.

CHOOSING YOUR THOUGHTS

Chapter 19

D o you choose your thoughts? You may think this question sounds weird. I mean, *of course* you choose your own thoughts… right? Still, do you need some time to think about that? Most people live by the opinions of others and allow others to choose their thoughts for them through conversation or the media. You have a choice to focus either on all the low vibrations in life or on the high vibrations of the each moment. Some people choose to expect limitations around each corner; others see the opportunities at every turn. What are you choosing to see? What are you choosing to experience in this life?

When something wonderful is happening, there are the people who say, "This won't last long." They expect a sudden, chaotic end to a glorious moment, because "the good things never last." There are people who choose to see happiness in all they encounter, and they receive just that. Then there are the people who choose to find fault in all they experience, and you know what? They, too, get exactly what they're looking for. Remember, all you think about, you *bring* about. The interesting thing is, at either end it always comes back multiplied.

The ones who find fault go about saying, "I'm down on my luck. It always happens to me. Things never work out for me." Then there's us—the ones good things are always happening for. We are "*those lucky ones.*" When something good happens, we look at it and say, "I knew something like that was going to happen; it turned out just as I thought." And so it is: as you believe, you will achieve.

A lot of people out there choose to reason or make excuses for why, once again, things didn't work for them. It's like saying that we would have to be "lucky" or that it won't likely work out, because "nothing ever does." That's what it's like when we walk in the lower vibration of energy: when we are expecting things not to work, they don't. Why would something happen when the thoughts and energy that are sent out to the universe are that it's not possible? Why should it happen, when we're carrying around an energy, a foregone conclusion, that it will not happen? We have rejected and shut down all opportunities for it to take form. We've quit before it ever started.

The people who bring their dream to reality often have visualized the outcome before it ever materialized in the physical realm. Their creative thoughts pull them along the path to their intention. They visualize the desired result so intensely, they can even see the stitching of the new outfit, or see themselves sitting on a new chair in the sunny breakfast nook of their new home before the ground is even broken to build it for them. Imaginatively experience your future before it ever appears. This will bring the thing you desire dramatically closer to you. You will begin to walk in the strengthening and empowering energy that brings people, places, and events into your life, because you begin to attract them just as a magnet attracts metal.

Intention is one of your main foundational blocks in manifesting your life. It works hand in hand with the will. The process of intention is, you let God, the universe, the Creator, know of your wish: "I wish for . . ." Then you ask God: "I ask for . . ." Next you must intend:

"I intend this in my life . . ." And eventually, you will act on your intentions. When you follow this, you have already won, even before you ever physically started, because of your intention to create, become, or accomplish. If you realize that you're off track, you don't just quit and say, "Luck wasn't on my side." Approach it from another angle, a different perspective. This will leave you with an entirely different perception of the possible.

Set a new action plan and embrace it, with will and desire for improvement in every dimension of what you intend to create. If your goal was to achieve something by a certain time or date and you happen to miss, simply take *action* by creating a new action plan for yourself and coming at it from a new angle and claiming your right to your intention. Your thoughts, when chosen well, have been laid on the foundation of will and intention, and the bonding mortar is gratitude. You are claiming your right to this life.

> *By thought all you want is brought*
> *to you, by action you receive it.*
> **—William James**

Don't make the mistake of thinking that the achievers, "the lucky ones," didn't have to go through what you did or didn't have it as tough as you. Most went through a lot more than we can imagine or even dare to think of ever having to endure. Winners stay in the game no matter what. They keep their focus on the intended point, and their will at a higher vibration, so they can resonate with their vision. They look for the good in every encounter. They learn from their failures and come back greater because, in reality, there is only feedback and opinions, which you can learn and grow from. The winners are learning from their experiences and taking opportunities to advance. An attitude of open interest allows you to welcome the challenges and be thankful for them, so you may grow to become a greater human.

Example

If you haven't heard of T. Harv Eker, he is a best-selling author and the founder and CEO of Peak Potentials Training. Harv's parents immigrated to Canada with almost no money at all, and throughout his childhood his family experienced financial scarcity. He worked since he was 13 years old, and when he went to university he decided he wanted to become a millionaire. He moved to the United States and tried different businesses that didn't give him the outcome he desired, until finally he opened this own business and achieved millionaire status.

Then, within two years of achieving his dream, he lost it all. But this was when his good fortune truly began, because it was only then that he realized that his thoughts were not aligned with his goals and dreams. Once he realized this, he managed to recover from his financial situation and bounced back to millionaire status within two and a half years. All Harv did was change his mind-set into a millionaire mind-set.

This is the power of your thoughts. Harv says, "We all have a blueprint for personal money and success." It is one that determines how much we achieve in life, and this blueprint is within us in our subconscious mind. He talks in his book and seminars about changing this blueprint to allow ourselves to achieve our goals, and although he mostly talks about it in terms of financial success, this will work for anything we desire in life. We know what's in our blueprint, because of the patterns and beliefs we have been living.

All these "living patterns" are expressed through our thoughts, emotions, and our actions. In everything we do, thoughts are *always* the first step. Anything that was ever accomplished in the history of the world, from a wooden spear to a supercomputer, started with a thought followed by an action. The Wright brothers thought of a self-propelled flying machine, Edison thought of a light bulb and moving pictures, and Rutherford thought of splitting the nucleus of an atom. The New World was discovered because Christopher Columbus thought there was something else beyond what the eyes could see, and the pyramids in Egypt stand because someone thought of them. Everything starts with a thought. Our thoughts guide our feelings and actions and are the most important components of our outcomes in life. Being aware of our thoughts makes all the difference. If T. Harv Eker hadn't thought about becoming a millionaire and kept that thought in his mind as a good idea and not just as an intention, he never would have become a millionaire—twice! This is a quote from his Millionaire Mind Intensive Seminar:

> So what is the difference between power thinking and positive thinking? The distinction is slight but profound. To me, people use positive thinking to pretend that everything is rosy, when they really believe that it's not. With power thinking, we understand that everything is neutral, that nothing has meaning except for the meaning we give it, and that we are going to make up a story and give something its meaning. This is the difference between positive thinking and power thinking. With positive thinking, people believe that their thoughts are true. Power thinking recognizes that our thoughts are not true, but since we're making up a story anyway, we might as well make up a story that supports us. We don't do this because our new thoughts are true in an absolute sense, but because they are more useful to us and feel a heck of a lot better than nonsupportive ones.

Experience

The decision to choose my own thoughts was a very simple one, one that didn't take any second thoughts on my part. But it took a bundle of attention at first—and still does at times—to be vigilant about my thoughts and see that they are truly mine, despite the media's and the surrounding energy's attempts to encroach.

After seeing how much pain there is out there, I came to the realization that even the best of us can fall into the trap of buying into someone else's reality. I choose not to put much stock in what is told, or the way it is told, in most of the media about local or world news. I try to get my information from reliable, unbiased sources. I get to choose my own thoughts on whether to let the information I receive shape my world. I still work daily on my personal development, since it is a never-ending process. Where I want to be on the playing field requires that I choose conscious thoughts, in the higher vibratory field, for every day I get to play.

> *The only limits you have are the limits you believe in.*
> **—Wayne Dyer**

My chosen conscious thoughts have taken me through all those physical rehabilitation years, brought me traveling and meeting people I would otherwise never have met, and given me new experiences to learn and grow from. When I place my focus on my personal intent and submerge myself in the vibrations of the higher-vibration people and fields I desire to play in, I get to move forward in huge strides and accomplish all I dream of and more. Here is how you consciously begin to choose your own thoughts and design your masterpiece as you choose it to be.

If I hadn't chosen my own thoughts, I would still be living with my left side paralyzed, not talking, lying in a bed at some medical institution. Besides being able to walk and talk, some other things I've received were meeting Bob Proctor, Mark Victor Hansen, Tony Robbins, Brendon Burchard, Paul Martinelli, and many others who are living the life they have designed by applying all the steps I'm sharing with you in this book. I can only imagine, as you have followed through on the exercises and have begun to apply them in your life, what dramatic changes and experiences may come your way.

Exercise

When you notice yourself following someone else's thoughts and doing what they are influencing you to do, think: why are you doing it? Are you just trying to keep the peace and their friendship? Have you noticed that you are on an emotional roller coaster because of the world news? Take this moment and ask yourself, *Who is this serving? Whose life am I living?* Is this stopping you from making decisions, or are you making choices for the wrong reasons—from fear, for instance? If you are going through any of these or similar situations, then they are having a greater influence on your life than you do. Begin today by re-creating yourself and choosing your thoughts. If it's a parent, lover, boss, the law, a therapist, or a friend or family member, they will *likely* have an invested caring interest in your life. If you tend to lead your life according to those opinions coming from other people, ask yourself, *Would the outcomes in my life be different if I began to live out my* own spirit's *feelings and opinions?* This is when *your thoughts* create things in your world. Start creating your own life!!

PART IV

ACTION

TRANQUIL OR CHAOTIC

How do you wish your life to be remembered? Picasso or paint-by-numbers? How are you living your life? Are you tapping into the dreams and talents that have been bestowed on you, and bringing your vision to a majestic reality? Are you manifesting your life, or letting it slide by and watching it as an unsettled observer? At some point during the day, take a look at the present moment to see how you can get the most from your personal experience. Look at all the ways you can learn and grow from it or by it. Take a step back; look at things from a different perspective. It's important to look at your life from another point of view. This opens doors that will give you opportunities to guide yourself through ways to improve this moment and your life in many areas. Can you see another outcome that would be a greater benefit to all it concerns or affects?

Now that you have taken the time to view your life from a different perspective, leaving you with a whole new perception, do you see how some focused thought would have created a beneficial outcome for all concerned, or an altogether different conclusion?

Stop stewing and start doing, TNT (today, not tomorrow).
—Denis Waitley

Action is powerful and has the creative ability to change your world entirely. Make a purposeful intention to act on your thoughts, and your future will become all you believe it can be. All that we are and have become or have ever done in our lives began with a thought. If you ever wish to change who or where you are in life, change your thoughts. Be thankful. Have faith, and make consistent improvements in your life. Watch the amazing attraction to this harmonious level of living and the passion you create. It will drive you to continue living the rest of your life on this plane of acceleration. Do you dare tap into your genius inside and create the Van Gogh image you wish to live by? Or will you sit back and merely exist by others' opinions and be content to paint by numbers? I chose to be a Van Gogh of my world; it will be a masterpiece of outstanding feats. Will yours?

At first it may seem impossible. Then it may
seem improbable. When one summons the
will, it soon becomes inevitable.
—Christopher Reeve

I learned from Bob Proctor that when you tap into the Six Faculties of the Mind (will, memory, perception, reason, intuition, imagination) consistently, you will begin to see good in every situation and find ways to learn and grow from everything you get to experience. Even when you use them all you will find that you benefit more from some than from others. These are all incredibly powerful when you have your purpose fueled with passion and faith.

Action has genius and creativity in it. "Do what you fear; action will conquer your fears." Leave the chaos behind and move toward a passionate life, bringing tranquility to the forefront of your living. This reminds me of something I heard from a person I deeply respect. He said, "We are human doings, not just human beings." He mentioned this as we were talking about how we could create more in our lives and design the life we choose to live. This was shortly after my fateful motorcycle ride. He had just quit a job that he had no passion for and that didn't fit his vision. At that time, I was in the initial process of redesigning my life, and I came to the conclusion that I wanted a regular dose of tranquility.

When you step into someone's energy and they are complaining or fussing, even if you have experienced something similar, your best action to take is to bring a constructive, empowering energy to him or her, in a higher vibration of empathy. Empathy is "the ability to understand and to be understanding of another person's emotions and situations. It is the ability, essentially, to relate to another's emotions." Many people confuse empathy with sympathy. Being sympathetic is having "the capacity for feeling another's unhappiness or misfortune, or the capacity to feel sorrow for another's suffering or misfortune."

The latter state, "sympathy," leaves you in a state of lower energy. Mostly, it brings on an enhanced version of chaos and more pain. But when you choose to be *empathetic,* you will be leaving others with the impression of increase and, potentially, ways to overcome their state of chaos. You leave them with thoughts of how to master the emotion or how they can increase their own life.

Now they can help others, as you just have, whether family, friends, or strangers, by all they have learned from enduring this challenge. If we choose, many of the challenges we sustain in life can be lessons that we cannot get or learn in such depth anywhere else. We can read all we wish on a particular subject and attend no end of classes and seminars, but we won't get the in-depth experience we get through enduring it and choosing to learn and win from it. With your experience, you are many leaps ahead of most teachings. Yes, it may still hurt, but now you have a choice to step into the tranquil energy and have it play a predominant role in your mind, enriching and empowering you by leaving the chaos behind.

Example

Many people would love to live the life Anthony Robbins lives. He truly is living the dream. And as people long to have a life like his, they don't stop to think that it wasn't always this way for him. Tony had to overcome many challenges before reaching the top. He went from rags to riches twice before becoming the person he is today, and before that, while he was growing up, his family faced financial issues while he had to deal with bullies at school. He didn't have a privileged life, and he had to work his way into what he is today.

The difference between Anthony Robbins and the people who dream of having a life like his is that through every challenge, he made a choice to learn from these tough times and build his character. From these experiences, Tony has done so much for others, it is astonishing what he has accomplished. Because he lived a chaotic life, he has become the "why guy." He has you explore where you are today, and he knows how to get you into peak state. He is known for his gift as a state inducer. He is the person who gets the call when the athlete is burning down on national television and he has to do something right now to get them back on top of their game because nothing else matters at that point. Through his difficulties, Tony found his passion, a passion he now shares with the world. His purpose is to help people figure out who they are so that they can place themselves as contributors to their own lives and the lives of others. His purpose is to show people how to understand and appreciate themselves and other people while finding tranquility in their life.

People of this mind-set, who do what Tony has done for others, receive as much or even more love and connection than they have given to others. This places Tony in a peak state of tranquility, when he sees what his vision and training have done for another life.

Tony always had big goals and the determination to make them happen. Before his twentieth birthday, he became a student of John Grinder, one of the founders of neurolinguistic programming. With this tool on his belt, Tony developed his own methods and helped so many people that he was called the "wonder kid." His life was getting better, and so were his finances, but somewhere along the way, Tony's life turned upside down again, and he ended up struggling with everything around him. This lasted until one day he realized that he had what he needed to change his life but wasn't choosing to use those resources. He decided to demand more of himself and never look back. He went from chaos to tranquility. All he did was *choose* the life he wanted to live.

What life do *you* choose to live? Are you living it?

Experience

My experience between chaos and tranquility manifested in a little different way—well, okay, a *very* different way. Let me tell you the experience. In the second year after the accident, my mother and I would go for walks in a ravine near a rehab center where I lived in Toronto, Ontario. Well, she would be walking, while I would be taking an extreme adventure, because there were times when I wasn't sure whether my left side would cooperate with me for the return trip home, or I would have to be carried all the way back. At this point, my body wasn't functioning smoothly in many ways, and it would shut down if I exerted myself by focusing on more than one or two functions at a time, such as walking and focusing on staying upright. Talking was often too much, and laughing could mean a total shutdown. You don't realize how much energy and bodily control laughing requires until you need 100 percent of your concentration just to stay upright. I had not received my voice back yet, so only small bursts of sound would come out, very quietly, almost as if I were gasping for air—like an infant trying to laugh.

On this particular occasion, when I was walking with my mother, we were joking around and laughing a lot as we walked along, which is a common occurrence when we spend time together. As I started to laugh harder and harder, I lost functionality in my legs and fell to my knees. (The chaos starts.) My mom was laughing so hard, she didn't see or hear me fall, so she kept on walking. By the time she noticed, she was already more than fifty feet away. My depth perception was distorted, so it looked like a hundred feet to me. I began heaving like a cat trying to bring up a fur all, and you know how ungainly a cat looks when doing that. Imagine a full-grown, thin, short guy in the middle of the park, on all fours, acting like a heaving cat. Can you picture that? I was rolling around on the ground with my feet and hands up in the air, laughing so hard I was gasping for breath and drooling. I'm sure I looked like a dog scratching its back on the ground, with its mouth wide open and its tongue hanging out. At that moment, two women walked by and saw me in that position.

So here's the dilemma: Do I get up and walk away feeling embarrassed, demeaned, and ashamed, or do I get up and say, "That was too funny! This is going to make a great story later."

Or do I choose tranquility? Well, instead of feeling bad, I chose tranquility—I chose to think it would make a good story. And now everyone knows my heaving-kitty story.

I have chosen tranquility over the chaos! Could you imagine where I would be if I had chosen to allow chaos, self-pity, and the ego to take control of this situation? Especially since people were walking by and looking at me with their cocked and eyebrows raised, looking at a man on all fours wobbling like a newborn fawn. Just imagine the bad feelings that would have plagued me. What good things would feeling bad about it have kept from my experience? This is something I know: that a lot of people allow chaos to affect their mental state, dragging them into a life that is not of their choosing.

Your life is worth every bit of what you can imagine or have ever imagined, and a great deal more. I am not saying this to make you feel good and sweet-talk you; I'm saying it because I know what you are capable of and what you are worth.

You are a tremendous spirit, created in the Lord's image, and he never makes mistakes or falters in what he does and why he does it. Where you are now or have ever been has all been a part of your greater plan for this life. The only thing holding you back from achieving all you can possibly imagine today or ever—yes, EVER—is the limits you have allowed to be impressed on your mind and spirit by your family, friends, the media, your surrounding environment, and, most of all, yourself! You can, at his moment, begin to feel the tranquility of the magnificent life of your choice.

Yes, what you are living and experiencing daily is all your choice, just as my life-changing incident was mine. I chose to place myself there, drive that fast, and think ignorant thoughts of invincibility. Every one of these choices was mine alone, just as it is my choice to write this for you, and just as it can be your choice to become every bit of the person you have ever imagined you could be. Step into your tranquil state of living today. Don't waste any more of your life and energy living less than what you desire.

Exercise

This will turn out to be exciting when you look back and say, "Why didn't I see that before?" Think of a time when you felt that your life was in chaos, out of control, out of your hands. Keep in mind, *what you focus on, you bring on*. Here is where you design your life as you choose it to be. Are you able to see any way you can benefit from that situation yet? Look at how it can serve you emotionally, mentally, or even spiritually. How can it bring you strength and support in other areas? How can you see that situation differently? What have you learned to do with your thoughts to serve *you*?

CANI: A COMMITMENT TO "CONSTANT AND NEVER-ENDING IMPROVEMENT"

Chapter 21

W hen you are constantly improving things in your life, something uncanny happens: as if by magic, your overall *quality of life* begins to improve. But this improvement will come to you only when you envision it as possible. Focus and action must be a daily walk. Anthony Robbins developed CANI (constant and never-ending improvement) after learning of the philosophy of Dr. Edwards Deming, an American who was a pioneer and leading expert in quality control. Dr. Deming's philosophy was simply to focus on constantly and never-endingly improving quality.

Tony Robbins adopted this in his own life and coined a word that would remind him of what he is really committed to. The word is "CANI." Many of the top manufacturers around the world use these beliefs and strategies every day. CANI is not about making big, groundbreaking changes all the time. It's the *little* changes that are the very foundation of this life-transforming habit. When living by the discipline of CANI and incorporating its strategy into your daily life, you will experience that consistent improvement that builds into a steady tide of ongoing fulfillment and power in every dimension of life. Make this your daily focus. Create a true commitment to CANI.

> *Convey the impression of advancement with everything you do, so that people shall receive the impression that you are an advancing man and that you advance all who deal with you.*
> **—Wallace D. Wattles**

Tell yourself that you deserve a consistently improving quality of life. Say to yourself out loud right now, "I AM WORTHY!" Repeat this to yourself often and daily! You will begin to feel the energy and power behind this word as you begin to believe it for yourself. When you ask for an increase of wealth in life, it is essential to have a belief in your own worth and to know that you deserve what you are asking for.

Improving on yourself in every little way you can is a constant walk in life. Think of waking up feeling this way, and if not, think of something you enjoy or are proud of. The feeling of worth will soon follow the feeling of joy. Find something that made you feel good, even if it was a while back. Relive it as completely as your memory allows. Feel all the joy, the giggles, the rush in life, and smile some while you're at it. Continue to walk through your day in the energy of your worth, and do this daily. It will help you live in the fullest sense of "CANI." This attitude shows the universe that you are ready to receive all you have asked for, and it puts out a signal of confidence, leaving an essence, an imprint, of increase in the quality of life on everyone you interact with.

Know what you are passionate about. The key here is to fit that passion into a purpose in every dimension of your life. Finding your purpose in life comes from asking yourself creative questions— questions that will give you answers to how you can consistently improve the quality of your life. What "CAN-I" do to improve? What "CAN-I" do that will change the negative patterns where I've been stuck into constructive, optimistic ones? Who "CAN-I" connect with or read about who will help me find some answers on how to live a fuller life—who can teach and guide me in how to manifest ways of possibility? As you begin to live your life this way, profound and amazing occurrences will happen, doors will open, lights will turn on, and your life will improve.

Start with small changes, like smiling at everyone you meet or finding something nice to say to others throughout your day. Don't be surprised if you find your family and friends commenting on the weird yet wonderful way you are acting. Weird to them, for you are beginning to act differently from what they are used to; wonderful because you are complimenting them; helping them; becoming more knowledgeable, understanding, and pleasant to be around. It will feel a little strange at first, but you will quickly become accustomed to the amazing feelings and opportunities that come to you.

> *Men acquire a particular quality by*
> *constantly acting in a particular way.*
> **—Aristotle**

People will suddenly appear to be friendlier, more cooperative, and more understanding. Going through life consistently focused on ourselves blocks our ability to see beyond our personal state. Adopting the mentality of CANI helps us become more aware of the world and all the energy it holds for each of us. The result, over time, is exponential personal growth benefiting every faculty of life. These faculties are memory, reason, will, intuition, imagination, and perception. Adopting the CANI philosophy in your life will bring about a passion to enrich yourself and all others along your chosen path. As we give off this passion, sending it out to the universe, it will always come back in abundance, enhancing and energizing all it touches.

Example

Dr. Edwards Deming experienced hardship early in life, yet soon he discovered how cooperation made life and work smoother and simpler. He saw the value of shared benefits by observing others and examining his own life. Deming dedicated his life to developing better ways for people to work together, within families, communities, government agencies, and large companies. He developed a system for individuals to plan and continually improve themselves and their relationships, processes, products, and services.

He developed his philosophy in the 1950s, by helping Japanese export industries recover from the devastation of the Second World War. Dr. Deming taught Japanese businesspeople an entirely new standard for conducting all commerce, and a new set of beliefs that, once put into practice, would bring to their companies quality and productivity they had never dreamed possible. This was the beginning of CANI—constant and never-ending improvement—the system developed by Anthony Robbins from Dr. Deming's teachings.

Dr. Deming's philosophy is one that requires cooperation and continual improvement. He said that if you wanted to change something for the better, to improve the quality in your life, your company, or your products, no *single action,* no matter how sweeping or dramatic, would do the job. He knew that real change would take a commitment to consciously and continuously improving *on every level* in life. He also understood that tone must "continually improve both the people in the system and the communication between the people." By doing this daily, gradually, you, too, will see an increase in the quality of everything you do.

> *The single biggest problem in communication*
> *is the illusion that it has taken place.*
> **—George Bernard Shaw**

When we finally understand that *everything* is better when we share and cooperate with others—when we want a higher quality of life for others—we discover a new world of possibilities and a newfound state of tranquility that changes our life forever. As we enrich other people's lives, we enrich our own as well. It is well worth the time and effort to give the extra mile every day. It does make a difference. Do it and enjoy the benefits!

Experience

As Anthony Robbins says, "You must constantly and never-endingly improve." My spirit remembered that statement while I was in an induced coma and immediately afterward, right when I woke up. My family had played his CDs over and over every day while I was in a coma, and I am eternally grateful they did. After ten days, I was brought back from the coma. Needless to say, I was excited to feel the essence of life again. I woke up deaf, blind, and mute. I'm sure my family thought those days were some of the most serene and peaceful days they had ever spent with me, because they could actually get a word in edgewise and I had no choice but to listen.

At best, I could sense my family's presence and feel what they were saying by the energy they were emitting, primarily through touch and thought. I felt lonely and incompetent because I couldn't communicate with anyone except by blinking—and even that was only after I finally learned how: once for yes, twice for no! After four weeks, my vision came back. I was nearsighted and could see only shadowy images in black and white.

Until I could move and walk with a walker (somewhere between six and seven months after waking), my daily exercise was CANI, every single step of the way. From the moment of my awakening, I felt a need to give love unconditionally, without expecting any reward or return of any kind. I still faced some mental and physical challenges and blocks, though I no longer choose to see problems—only the possibilities that lie within them. By using CANI, I can consistently improve all facets of my reality. The doctors told me I would never walk again, talk again, eat solid food, or move my left side. But I came around to doing all these things because I made a choice to live by the strategies and standards of CANI, combining that with a strong faith in our Creator. I was walking and talking within seven months, and I'm getting better daily. I'm already riding my bike, and soon I'll be running again! How's that for constant and never-ending improvement?

Exercise

I *challenge* you to do this exercise for seven days: Tune in to your thoughts and feelings constantly, and don't act on any negative thought that comes up. These thoughts may enter your mind more often than you would like, but you don't have to entertain them. You can just acknowledge them and, without fighting them, let them go by. Whatever comes to your mind that is negative, don't act on it. If you do, then you must start your seven-day challenge over again. This will place you in a mind-set of always looking for the greater good and holding yourself to a higher vibration so that you improve consistently. Record your experiences. It is vitally important that you follow through on this, for it will change every facet and dimension of your life.

Chapter 22

JUST GIVE

Our Creator says: "Give and it shall be given unto you." The law of circulation states that all things in the universe are always circulating and are ever-expanding. What you give to one person will likely come back to you from a different source. So you can forget about giving with the expectation that this same person will give it back to you. It will definitely come back to you manyfold, but from someone else—or even several someone elses. This is just the law of cause and effect in action: the universe always mirrors back to you whatever you do. The law of circulation also states, "Give unconditionally, while being true to yourself and others and without depleting yourself, just because it feels good to give." In other words, don't take from someone to give to someone else, or to enrich oneself. However, the power and passion with which you give will always return tenfold.

To receive everything, one must open one's hands and give.
—Taisen Deshimaru

It is human nature to give and feel joy. It's in our DNA to care for and support another and to experience fulfillment from doing so. It is in the nature of us all to care for and bring joy to another, whether that other is from the same bloodline or is just a life that needs care and support. To assist, guide, protect, love, and create is the nature of life. We are creatures of compassion; we thrive on personal contact and on knowing we are of value and have worth. The wild part of all this giving stuff is, the more you do for others, the more expanded your life becomes. We are creative and ever-expanding spirits. Nothing in life feels as good as giving just because you can and want to.

Have you ever smiled at a toddler and had them look back with a grin from ear to ear, or watched them giggle and hide? Hmm-m, what a feeling! It isn't easy to describe the true essence of the feeling. Can you recall a moment when someone gave you a gift that you thought was the whole world, and it made you want to give back an equal if not greater feeling of joy? Do you remember making your parents something at school—a painting, drawing, or sculpture in modeling clay? It may have been a creation of multiple pieces of colored paper, pipe cleaners glued together, or a crayon rainbow. Do you remember the excitement you felt over giving it to them? I'll bet you were jittering with excitement, dancing all over. Mom or Dad was asking, "What do you have, sweetie?" And you could barely contain yourself. If you look back, you'll find you have a memory of doing something just like this.

What happened to that all excitement we had for life? Where did it go? What happened to giving for no reason? Why did it stop? A friend of mine told me a story about a woman she knew who decided to do a random act of kindness every day in 2010. One day she was at a gas station, ready to pay, and decided to pay for the guy behind her as well. It dumbfounded him. He kept asking her why—he just couldn't believe that a random act of kindness was possible. We are so conditioned these days that when someone does something kind for us, we suspect them of wanting something in return. It doesn't have to be this way; we can do something for another person just because it pleases us!

> *The habit of giving only enhances the desire to give.*
> —Walt Whitman

A smile or a kind word goes a long way. Even if it isn't reciprocated, it will bring the recipient joy and affect you in a positive way. You will feel as though someone just complimented you. To create the future you want, begin to adopt this habit of giving, if for no other reason than just because you can. Use a smile or a kind word. They're easy, they cost nothing, and you have an abundance of them. Sometimes I have smiled so much, my cheeks got sore and I had to stop. You may have experienced something similar before. The good news is, I have never heard of anyone whose face broke from smiling too much or too often. Watch what happens! You will be amazed at the abundance of good things that begin to come your way as you continue to walk and live in a higher energy!

Example

Mother Teresa is well known for all the work she did in India and around the world. For Mother Teresa, life itself was all about giving. She decided to become a nun when she was eighteen years old, and a few months later she was sent to Calcutta, India. The suffering and poverty around her left a deep impression on her, and she traded the safety of the convent to work among those who needed her the most, outside its walls. She was a woman of faith—and also of action. She wrote down everything she was inspired to do, and when the moment came when someone asked for her plans in writing, all she had to do was hand them over. She was well prepared. With no resources other than her faith, she accomplished what most would have thought impossible. Mother Teresa had the intention of doing something. She didn't know how it was going to happen, yet she had the conviction, the faith, that somehow it would. And it did! Others joined her to help the poor, and sometime after that she had a new religious order serving the people. She treated everyone as if they were Jesus himself, in need of her help, and she let her love overflow into every other human being she encountered.

Mother Teresa said, "I aim to help the naked, the hungry, the homeless, the crippled, the blind, the lepers, and all the people that feel unwanted, unloved, and uncared for throughout society." This was her purpose in life. Mother Teresa's purpose began to attract financial support from many different corners of the world. As soon as she made the choice to focus her thoughts on creating something, she had the faith that it would happen, and then she took any action she could to make it happen. She then became very successful at having her thoughts become things.

> *Spread love everywhere you go. Let no one*
> *ever come to you without leaving happier.*
> **—Mother Teresa**

Mother Teresa started her work in Calcutta and then went on to Venezuela and Rome. It didn't take long, with a determination as strong as hers and with God's guidance, to open convents in almost all the Communist countries, including the Soviet Union, Albania, and Cuba. She was known internationally for her giving nature, peacefulness, and energy. Both governments and civilian organizations honored Mother Teresa. The United Kingdom and the United States each repeatedly granted her awards for her constant work. She would receive tenfold what she asked from governments, organizations, and civilians, because she would use it only to improve others' lives and circumstances.

She devoted her whole life to giving, and although she received many rewards for her work, her biggest reward was putting a smile on everyone else's face. There is no better example of giving than the life of Mother Teresa.

Experience

Before my motorcycle crash, I was living a challenging yet good life. It was a little chaotic, though I had lots of fun. I owned two rapidly growing businesses, which afforded me a life with choices. I traveled some, bought most of the things I wanted, and did most of the things I wanted to do, when I chose to do them. Giving was a part of my life, but not to the extent it is today.

The accident turned all that upside down. As you read in my story, not much on my body was functioning after the crash. After you have been "to hell and back" or "as close as one can get," you tend to have a different perspective on life. One day you have all your faculties, and the next day you wake up to realize that you're missing most of them and that the few you still have aren't working well. You quickly realize that you should have been more grateful for all you did have, while you had it. You quickly regret every moment that you were not thankful for ALL that you had, when you had it.

If you really think it's your right to walk, talk, see, hear, or feel, then respect what faculties you have now and be grateful for every one of them, even if they aren't functioning as well as they might. You don't know that you are always going to have them, and let me assure you, if you ever have to do without any of them, even for a short time, you will miss them dearly.

> *Give love and unconditional acceptance to*
> *those you encounter, and notice what happens.*
> **—Wayne Dyer**

In the hospital, I asked our Creator to guide me through every walk I would take—to be my eyes when I could not see, my ears when I couldn't hear, and my voice when I couldn't speak. From day one, every baby step I took was a chore, but I had divine support and infinite patience. One of the first functions that returned was the ability to smile. I had always thought a smile was a simple expression to show my love and excitement for life. Then one day I realized it was not a wise thing to do while lying on my back. I could not for the life of me figure out why, when I heard people talking, it sounded as though I was underwater. It turned out that as I was smiling to show my love and gratitude in having them around, my ears would fill up with "laughter liquid." Because of the paralysis to my face, I couldn't keep my lips closed, which meant I was often drooling without knowing it.

So now that you know of this publicly frowned-upon challenge I was faced with, the question for you is, did I allow it to control me and my options for my future? Did I choose to stay in some of the lowest and most destructive energy vibrations one could ever entertain? Or did I choose tranquility and design my life as I saw it becoming? Negative emotions, being low in energy, only weaken us and generate illness and disease in the body. What do you think I chose?

Once I could smile, life was much better. I could communicate in more ways than just blinking! Going through the rest of rehab was still a challenge, but I always found a way to smile, glisten, or show love and appreciation to all I came in contact with. It's amazing how far a smile can take you and what it will say when truly expressed. A vision began to form with my rehab. My vision and purpose that I had been blessed with was to give back to others all I was being given, and then some.

So how does all this fit in with "Just give"? For one thing, the nurses were extra nice to me. They helped me whenever I asked. Often, nurses stopped in to just say, "Hello, hope you have a good day, Daniel." All the surgeries I needed were scheduled quickly. When a several-month waiting period was normal, I was in within days or a few weeks at the most. Whenever I needed something, I truly didn't have to wait long. I am blessed with a family that loves me, but a lot of what was done for me was done by the nurses, because I showed respect and gratitude for their actions and gestures. It plays in perfect harmony with "Give, and it will be given to you. A good measure, pressed down, shaken together and running over, will be poured into your lap. For with the measure you use, it will be measured to you" (Luke 6: 38). All I had of myself to give at this time was good humor and a high level of energy (when I was awake).

Yes, there were times when I was in pain and discomfort, really confused and shaken up. It is in these chaotic times that giving unconditionally of yourself can make a world of difference for you. I knew I must give something, even if I had very little to give. The universe saw that I was giving of myself for the betterment of another. Whether it was a lot or a little, it was with good intention, and it was all I had at the time.

I am certain that if I had moved in a destructive or selfish way, the effort and care put into my well-being would have not been even half what it was. Those nurses made sure I was in good hands and well taken care of. They were truly awesome. My love for them is unconditional. Because of this, I have been blessed over and over with a strength of will that shocks even me at times. By doing something as simple as a partial smile (with or without the attractive drool!), I received from my family and other caregivers all that I required and more. It has changed my world! This is why I must do all I can to give back to the world, especially to the medical and rehabilitation community!

> *Your circumstances do not determine what is in*
> *you to give; they reveal what is within you to give.*
> **—Wayne Dyer**

Exercise

When you do a good deed for someone for no reason, it changes your life. Give to others just because you can. It can be something as simple as going out of your way and holding a door open for somebody, or stepping aside and letting them in front of you in a line. To do this is to leave somebody feeling better than they did before. What do you wish to attract to you? When someone does this for you, how does this make you feel? Look at how simple it is to feel grateful in life and to leave someone else in a state of gratitude. Just imagine how much say you have in the design of your community. Start now doing something for those around you. I guarantee you, it feels fantastic!

BE THE
CHANGE YOU
WISH TO SEE

Chapter 23

B ecome the magnificent person God created you to be. Set the example. "Do unto others as you would have them do unto you" (Luke 6: 31). As you do this, people will begin to notice a difference in you, and they will begin walking in a higher frequency just so they can be nearer you. They will also notice that they feel better around you because you have a "good energy." This will initiate some changes in them, and it will be the change you wish to see. This will build confidence in your conviction, enabling you to accomplish much more now that you have begun to design this life of your choosing. You will experience doors opening, opportunities arising, and paths clearing so that you may accomplish your purpose.

People often look outside themselves for reasons why they are not achieving their desired results or living a life of their choice. To find the true source, you need only look inside yourself to find the true reason that things in your life are the way they are. The law of attraction, one of the fundamental aspects to living a life by design, explains that everything created in the outside world is the result of what takes place internally. Being the change you wish to see in the world starts with your taking full responsibility for everything that is happening in your life.

Believe in what you can do. It will become you.

Remember that everything you think about and talk about, you bring about. Your thoughts and actions, since the day you were born, have brought you to this very moment you are in, and will continue to manifest your reality for the rest of your life. By the same logic, every decision you make going forward will also affect that same reality. You choose whether it is a positive or negative result and whether you walk away enriched or depleted. If you want to change some things in the world, you must first change some things in you. If you want people to smile, smile at them first. If you want people to talk nicely to you, talk nicely to them. This will bring about the change you wish to see.

The first law of supreme influence states, "I create my reality." Creating your life by design requires your full ownership and total personal accountability for where you are right now. By accepting that you are fully "at cause" for your life, you can access the wisdom to recognize how your moment-to-moment thoughts, words, and actions create the results you experience.

This personal journey you are on is about giving all you can to yourself and others, openly and honestly and with love. To improve your world, you must _live_ in it, not just _exist_ in it. You have a tremendous power to create your life as all you envision it to be. Be determined to sculpt this vision into reality. What change do you wish to see?

Do what you can, with what you have, where you are.
—Theodore Roosevelt

Living in this reality may be a challenging concept to wrap your mind around, but like it or not, each of us is the director and engineer of the results we experience in life. You are the creator of your surroundings and your future. Life around you is a mirror image of who you are. You will attract a modified version of the same actions you present or give to others. For if you wish your environment to change, first change your attitude. Every thought we have, every word we speak (whether internally or out loud), and every action we take is like planting a seed that will develop and grow when the appropriate conditions arise. Like a gardener carefully planting what will be the next harvest, we reap the effects of having planted the seeds of past thoughts and behaviors.

To bring about positive change in the world, we need to pay more attention to the results and focus less on the reasons why things didn't turn out as we had planned. We must engage not only with the outer world but also with our inner world. If we want to see greater awareness in the world, we have to cultivate awareness in ourselves. If we want to see more harmony and less strife, we need to become more masterful at handling our emotions and learn to respond to frustrations with more patience and kindness than we do at present.

Most people do not live on purpose. Take a moment and think about how often you recognize someone giving reasons in the absence of results. Have you done this? Do you know someone who, no matter what is happening in their life, will tell you that it is not their fault? People who don't understand their ability to create their own reality tend to blame their environment for the results they get. Anytime you give a reason for not getting the result you wanted, even when it seems to be real and true, you are saying that what is happening outside you is more powerful than your ability to transform it. And that is the furthest thing from the truth!

Human behavior is very predictable. The average person, upon perceiving that someone is doing them wrong, will react in one of these ways: blame others, deny the situation, or justify the situation. People try to excuse their own behavior by denial or justification, or else they put the responsibility outside themselves by blaming someone or something else. But aren't all these actions simply different ways of producing reasons that things didn't work out? Taking ownership for your thoughts, words, actions, and everything that is happening within your personal universe raises your consciousness. When you are the cause for what occurs in your life, it delivers power to you, supporting you on your journey to be the change you wish to see in the world. The only true thing you can change is you.

Example

Mahatma Gandhi was the most respected spiritual and political leader in India. He helped free the Indian people from British rule, through nonviolent resistance, and is honored by Indians as the father of their nation.

Gandhi left India to become a lawyer in London. When he returned to India, he was disappointed by the lack of working opportunities, so he accepted a job with an Indian law firm in South Africa. It was there that his life changed and he became a leader against discrimination. He turned into the man who became the change he wanted to see in the world.

He followed the principles of courage, nonviolence, and truth. He understood that our behaviors are more important than our achievements, and because of this belief, he promoted nonviolence and civil disobedience as the tools to accomplish political and social goals. Gandhi returned to India, where he became the leader of the Indian nationalist movement. His nonviolent convictions were so strong that he rejected violence even when he was attacked and beaten for protesting. He would simply say, "May God bless you all." As his attackers started to realize that he would not retaliate, the violence against him stopped. Because he was peaceful no matter the circumstances, he created peace in his world. Maybe the whole planet didn't become peaceful, but peace manifested in his own world. That should also be our goal. Others will follow our example, and peace will spread.

Dream as if you'll live forever. Live as if you'll die tomorrow.
—Mahatma Gandhi

Gandhi fought for all sorts of legislation to free the Indians from oppression. He was so imbued with the spirit of his personal intention that he did not fall prey to egotistical fantasies of his own greatness but stayed true to his convictions.

A young Hindu radical shot Gandhi, yet at the moment of his death, he recognized God in the eyes of his assassin. His last word was "Ram," a name of God, which refers to authenticity, reminding us to remain connected to our true nature—the character that we create for ourselves. The challenge comes in deciding who or what it is that we wish to create. You don't get much more authentic than that.

Experience

Before the crash, I was nice to people, but I wasn't necessarily a nice guy. I wasn't so much a "be the change you want to see" person. I was more like a "complain and manipulate to get the change you want to see" person. A lot of the time, I was just being extra friendly and nice because it was the easiest way to get what I wanted.

> *A problem cannot be solved at the level*
> *of consciousness in which it occurs.*
> **—Albert Einstein**

The "being the change you want to see" part is actually all on *this* side of the accident. The passion I have to give out more love, trust, and honesty than I ever did before has empowered me with an intention of becoming more loving and appreciative for life. I am still growing and will be learning more and more about the true me for as long as I breathe. The wonderful part of seeing yourself as "being the change you want to see" is that you are never finished. You always have goals to set, to become more of the authentic you in every facet of your life. I live by this plan, and I am willing and open to grow in depth and meaning.

I am a loving spirit of intent that can do well only through giving, creating, helping, loving, guiding, teaching, and doing everything that my soul intends for others. My vision is to coach and teach others how to create exceptional relations, both personal and professional, and how to tap into the power of intention and guide their lives along the path of their choosing. Achieving this is not the simplest of tasks. I work on this and on myself every waking, sleeping, or meditating moment. This is the fun part of living a life of continuous growth: it's not just about seeing every day as a new start to life; it's about being aware of life and living *every moment* with intent, passion, and purpose.

If, at this moment, you are only scratching the surface of life's energy source, you are still further ahead than you were before. For now you have begun to live and feel life and its endless potential that we all have at our fingertips. The more you immerse yourself in it and the more you put it into practice, the more aware you will become and the more of it you will bring into your reality. That has been my experience, which is why I am so excited to have the opportunity to experience every new day. This is why, if I have a less-than-ideal day, I anticipate and intend tomorrow in such detail that it gets me excited to experience it. It doesn't matter what is going on around you, or the thoughts others try to impose on your life. When you place the intention, fueled with kindness, passion, and purpose, in front of any challenge, you empower yourself in any situation. This occurs because you are energized with the powers of intention—with love, kindness, joy, beauty, receptivity, expansiveness, and abundance. You will be acting rather than reacting.

I smile at everyone I meet. It brings in lots of return smiles. I do my best to be the change I want to see. My mind-set is to make sure that everyone feels better just from knowing me.

If you are powered by intention and guided by your mind-set, your possibilities are endless. When you harness this vision of possibility, you will expose your magnificent self and come to the realization that nothing happens by accident or coincidence.

Exercise

Imagine where you want to be five years from now. What do you feel needs to change around you or within you? This is your time to be the change you want to see, by beginning to act as you want others to act toward you and around you. Start today. Describe how you would like others to treat you, by writing it down and reading it back to yourself. Once again, nothing ever happens by coincidence, and the world reflects a precise image of what we give to it. Start today by treating the world exactly the way you wish to be treated.

OPPORTUNITY TO CHANGE

Chapter 24

Your outer world is a direct reflection of your inner world. Think of life as a bank—better yet, as an investment account. The investment you deposit into the account is what you put into life: your feelings, actions, time, energy, and thoughts. The "return" on your investment is what you receive back that exceeds what you have put in. As people around you act or react to you, be aware that this return on investment depends on what you have put into your account. Our outer world is a direct reflection of our inner world. You attract back to you, most of the time, in greater amounts than you give.

> *We must all suffer from one of two pains: the pain*
> *of discipline or the pain of regret. The difference is,*
> *discipline weighs ounces while regret weighs tons.*
> **—Jim Rohn**

This is the opportunity you have been waiting for. You called for it; now it is here. Now is the time to speak into your life ALL that you have been thinking of, dreaming of, wishing for. Commit to the emotion of gratitude. Be grateful for all you have and ever imagined becoming in your life. When your intention is of a high vibration, you will begin to acquire whatever it takes to achieve your desired goals. You will begin to live your word, and everyone around you will see this. You will notice that people, places, things, and events come into your life at the most opportune moments.

First believe it, and then you will see it. Believe it in your thoughts as though they already existed, because they do! As I said earlier, all that we are seeking is seeking us in return, with equal intensity. The more open you are to receiving your dreams, the more open your dreams are to receiving you. This knowledge should give you the courage and the desire to follow through with all your plans and dreams for this life. If you find you are not receiving, have more faith and gratitude. Visualize your purpose with greater intention and generate the emotion to go with it, and it will come to you. Keep believing, and you will get it!

> *Self-talk is the strongest self-development*
> *habit you have with which to build yourself.*

Feel the joy, happiness, and fulfillment that come with achieving your goal. Feel it as though it were here in your presence as you read this. Get excited. Get emotional. Allow yourself to feel as though you had already achieved it. Talk about it as though you had already received it. Think about it in the present tense. Think about all you will do with it when you bring it into your reality. Just imagine yourself wearing that outfit, driving that car, petting that new puppy, on the deck of the cruise ship on your dream vacation. Envision everything: the breeze in your hair, the feeling of those new shoes, the joy your new pet brings to you. Allow your inner vision to run wild as though your imaginings were real. Your subconscious does not distinguish between reality and envisioning. It will automatically begin to release the energies throughout your body so that you carry with you a different persona, stature, and energy. This is your opportunity to change. Grab it while you can!

When you step into your dreams and passions you will begin to move in the attractive energy that you have heard about and that I have spoken about throughout this book. As I said, like a magnet, you will attract all you need.

Belief creates behavior, and behavior creates results.

Example

We all have the opportunity to change, and each day is a fresh opportunity to start anew. It doesn't matter how challenging it may seem, whether we have the resources at hand, or what others tell you. What matters is what you believe and what you decide to make of your life. Here is the story of Troy Evans, a man who was sent to prison for multiple armed bank robberies. Troy was a living a life surrounded by notorious criminals such as Timothy McVeigh and Terry Nichols. When Troy was sentenced to thirteen years behind bars, he decided not to waste any more of his life. Now, you may be thinking, what can a man do in jail other than waste his time? After all, isn't that his punishment for the crimes he committed? Well, Troy managed to turn this negative circumstance into a positive one. He decided to try to become a better man. And this is what we all need to remember: we can always, no matter what our circumstance are or how we got into them, change our lives around for the better. It's all in the attitude—that belief within ourselves of what is possible for us. In education, Troy found his chance to change, and after six months of work filling applications, writing essays, and pleading for a chance, he got his first scholarship to take one class. He was released seven and a half years later, with two degrees and a GPA of 4.0, and his name on the dean's and president's lists.

You overcome old habits by leaving them behind.
—Wayne Dyer

Today Troy is a motivational speaker, and he shares his story so we, too, can escape the "prisons within ourselves" by overcoming adversity, adapting to change, and realizing our full potential.

Take a look at all the ways you can help, guide, teach, or become a role model for those around you with what you have just learned. Troy didn't just gain some insight; he transformed himself and got inspired to make a difference for the betterment of others, especially youth, because he had chosen to learn and grow from his personal challenges

Experience

Before my motorcycling incident, you could have described some of my character attributes with words such as "self-centered," "greedy," "uncaring," and "selfish." I looked at people, things, and situations in terms of what was best for me, or how I could benefit from it, while maybe helping you out. Any help I gave, I gave when I felt like it. It wasn't something I focused on a lot.

When they let me wake up from the coma, that all changed. Getting excellent treatment from doctors and staff at the hospitals and rehabilitation centers, and seeing how my family went out of their way to make my journey to renewed health the best it could possibly be, motivated me to become the humble, kind, and giving person I believe I am today.

> *Do not be shaped by this world; instead be*
> *changed within by a new way of thinking.*
> **—Romans 12:2**

As time went on I found out that I didn't need to be who I had been before, that I could be anybody I wanted to be. It just happened to take a massive, life-changing injury for me to wake up to it. I was living a decent life, but the biggest part of life was missing, and I didn't know what it was, because I was too caught up in the material world and in myself. I know this was a fact of that life, because I managed to get myself hurt many times. All through this time, I had many opportunities to change myself, yet I ignored them. It wasn't until I nearly lost my life that I came to the realization that I wasn't the axis that this world spins on. The only world I was the center of was my own little universe, and it didn't have any guidance or balance in it. It looked like one of those bobble heads that people stick under the rear window of their cars. What I have finally learned—and I am so glad I did—is that anybody who thinks the world revolves around them misses a whole universe of opportunities and experiences that would otherwise be available for them. And most of the time, a feeling of emptiness is the result.

I was in pursuit of success, and I aimed for achievement in obtaining a certain level of quality in life. This is where self-imaging comes in. I always wanted to be the best at whatever I did, and I had a need to outdo the next competitor. In aiming for this, most of the time I accomplished what I was aiming for, and when I didn't, I was generally way over my head and would physically smash myself up pretty hard, so that I had to take some time out of that life. During the time-out phases, I would fall behind, or at least not progress as far as I wanted. So I went back out, pushing myself harder than before, until again I landed in a crumpled heap. I obviously didn't take seriously the opportunities to change, because I was so ruled by my ego. I thought that an opportunity to change meant to do it better and learn not to crash so much next time.

This wasn't just with the sports. I did this in every facet of my life. Build it, become it, then crumple it! Then do it all over again. That's why I didn't find it easy to change. That's who I was at the time—or, at least, who I thought I was. I created the conflicting and conflicted person whom I was forever battling inside.

Success is not to be pursued; it is to be attracted by the person we become.
—Jim Rohn

Today I go out of my way to help, guide, and nurture anyone who is in need and is open to getting assistance. My primary focus is through the medical community, which is the largest hands-on customer service industry in the world. I get to speak at many venues about all that is possible, human potential, the purpose of intention, and the power of the mind-set. I decided to write this book about how this has changed my life. When you live on purpose, it will leave an impression on you to improve your life constantly. And this will give you an experience of fulfillment through *service* by giving back to all people and to our world. If you ask my friends and family, they will tell you that I took the opportunity to change, and that it has been for the better!

Exercise

There is something you have wanted to change for a while now, and you haven't. Now is the time! Think of that one challenge bigger than the ones you have been working on through this book. You will change it! Start thinking of the ways you want it to change. Now that you have all the small steps to bring this change about and you have practiced them throughout your journey with this book, begin now, either with small steps or with a solid decision. You have this guide in your hand. What is it that you intend to change?

CREATING
SELF-WEALTH
AND
SELF-WORTH

Chapter 25

The most powerful and influential habit affecting your self-wealth and self-worth—for good or ill—is your self-talk. Indeed, good self-talk is one of the most important habits you can cultivate in your life, since it puts you in the higher energy vibration that brings your goals within reach.

You must demonstrate to yourself and those around that you are successful and prosperous in your mind and spirit. As I never tire of saying, you must believe it, see it in your mind's eye, and feel it emotionally before you experience it physically. It will come to you, and with every thought you will draw it closer as you continue to believe that it is yours. It makes no difference whether you are anywhere near your goal yet, whether you have any useful connections, or whether you can even see a way to reach it. It is by your belief in your own worth that you will succeed. Once you believe in your own worth and start consistently seeing yourself where you desire to be, you will become abundantly prosperous—and stay that way throughout your life.

Live your life with intention, vision, and purpose as you push through the challenges that come your way. In doing this, you are proving to yourself that you can become all that you have ever visualized and imagined becoming. As I said before, you become what you think about all day long. So what are you thinking about?

What you plant in your mind and think about regularly will necessarily return with the same intensity you nurtured it with. If you are thinking consistently about a worthwhile, concrete goal, which is the first step, you are bringing it much closer to you. Every time you think about and imagine what you desire and what you intend to do with it when it comes to you, how it will make life better, what it will help you create or become, you are working on the first step. Second, begin to *take action* on your desires, and you will achieve them. This means go out and look at it, touch it, walk through your dream house, test-drive that car, create vision boards, meditate, envision it in your possession. Why? Because it will raise your vibrations so that *you* begin to resonate with your vision. Because that is what you are thinking about and speaking about, and that is what you will *bring* about. Conversely, if you have no goals, no vision or focus in your life, and intend nothing in particular for yourself, you will get exactly what you are thinking about: nothing in particular! If you think of nothing, you become nothing more than you are. In creating self-wealth and self-worth, the foundational cornerstone is what we think about day in and day out and how we think about it. It is a law of nature—just as real and dependable as gravity. Test it; it's there. Though invisible, it is as real as the air you breathe.

Picture yourself already achieving your goal. Picture the things you will do when you achieve your goal. Visualize now and every day how you will act, talk, and move. Begin right this second, exactly where you are.

Goals are the blueprint for your life.

If you want *better* in your life, set better goals—or, at least, start by setting *some* goals. You are where you are, because that is exactly where you want to be, whether you admit it or not. It is what you have been thinking about and speaking about. Like it or not, if you thought and talked about it, you created it. Whether you are, in this moment, perfectly healthy or physically, mentally, or emotionally challenged, this law holds true equally for us all. If you are not ready to believe this yet, just *pretend* to believe it and you'll be amazed by the changes that happen. When you follow through with the steps provided in this book, you can't help but attract to yourself the desired outcomes. Many people have proved this law over and over, and now I am living the proof of what these actions can manifest for you. The awesome part here is, that the more I develop and experience my own self-worth, the more the standards of my self-wealth rise. Do these things, and it is a given that the financial, health, career, family, spiritual, and social wealth will begin to flow in proportion to the respect you have of yourself.

I will now be up in your face for a moment. Everything we have encountered in this life since our birth, we called into our lives. Now, if you were born with a debilitating challenge, your starting point may be different, but the rest is all your call. From where you are now, all you choose to become and create in your life is your choice. You choose what you focus on. This is your life, your world! It's the life of your choice!

Life is an exciting adventure, a wondrous journey. Be wise. Choose to live a life of wonder, joy, and bliss.

> *If standard of living is your major objective,*
> *quality of life almost never improves. But if*
> *quality of life is your number one objective, your*
> *standard of living almost always improves.*
> **—Zig Ziglar**

Example

Joe Vitale was not always the confident, secure man you have seen on TV's *The Secret, The Compass,* and other programs or at one of his events. He has overcome living in poverty. Over thirty years ago, he was homeless for a decade. A struggling author and speaker, he was depressed, suicidal, and living in a state of desperation.

He went from that bleak existence to living a luxurious lifestyle and having numerous books out and being on influential television programs. How did he do all this? He followed his passion, and when that passion wasn't turned on he lit it up by finding ways to get excited. And this excitement gave him the drive to seek out his purpose. Joe concluded that his enthusiasm and following his heart always lit him up and set a fire under his butt to move forward. Joe knows that at times life gets bumpy, especially when we have limiting beliefs that don't support us. What he has found that works best for him is intentional self-talk using the empowering word.

When you are talking to yourself about what you want to do and will do, you're not frustrating yourself with all the things you dislike or don't want to happen. Instead, you are constructively building yourself up with empowering self-talk—self-talk that can guide you and boost your confidence and your opportunities. Joe has found his purpose through odd "coincidences" and has gone on in life to great fame and success. He is considered one of the top copywriters and most successful and respected marketers in the world.

Self-respect is a question of recognizing
that anything worth having has a price.
—Joan Didion

During the rough times, Joe had no clue about the talents and attributes lying dormant inside him. He never suspected that they would someday rise to the surface, turn everything in his life around, and make him a leader in the field of self-advancement.

The purpose of this book is to give you this opportunity to learn from all the lessons that people like Joe and me went through, and be guided to a higher quality of life without having to go through it all yourself. Learn from our mistakes and save yourself years and tears.

Experience

As you follow what you are learning in this book, you will see more and more daylight, no matter what sorts of challenges you are facing. While I was recovering, I found that most people around me who where facing tough challenges had an "I give up" attitude. Either they didn't have any desire to move forward in life or, if they did, they wouldn't take action to move ahead. If I had believed what the doctors told me, what I read and was told about brain injuries, and what others would say when they thought I couldn't hear or understand them, I would have ended up living in a long-term care facility, in a vegetative state, being fed through a tube to my stomach. That is precisely where I would be if I had allowed the "I give up" attitude of those around me to invade my thoughts and self-belief. It's no easy task to dismiss what comes in from the external world, especially when you are lying in a bed with no movement in half of your body, muted and not being able to eat. At that moment, what you need to believe is that you can get better, even when you have no idea how or when it is going to happen. Now, don't get me wrong: it's important to follow medical advice—after all, I went through many surgeries, physical rehabilitation, speech therapy, and occupational therapy—but you don't need to let the thoughts and words of others lead you to an "I give up" attitude that can paralyze your life. If you are breathing, if your heart is beating, then there is hope for something better. Throughout my journey through recovery and healing, I had to push the limits many times. Too often, the doctors and therapists would repeat, more times than I wanted to hear, that I couldn't do things or that I was not going to get much better. What did I do then? I told them that I respected their opinions but I was sticking with mine, that I would still push myself more every time I had therapy—and that I would do it with or without their help. Of course, it would be better to have their help, and most times they agreed to help me despite their own skepticism. I know I had the greatest health-care team I could ever have, because they opened their minds to the possibility of more, and they gave it a try. I also trained many hours when not in therapy. I pushed as much as I possibly could, because I knew that it was the only way I could gain mobility in the left side of my body and have a coherent thought. And I made it! I can walk, talk, and eat solid foods once again.

Other people's opinions or assumptions are just that: a personal view, attitude, judgment, or assessment that belongs to that particular person or group of people. It is their belief of what they think is possible in their own life, projected onto you and your life. They are treating you as if you were their mirror, which you are not! You are uniquely *you,* and you get to choose what you want your life to be. You decide what to take into your mind and what to leave out. You will go as far as you believe you can go. Believing in yourself and your abilities, and knowing that you deserve what you believe in, is what gives you self-worth. You are the one who determines your worth. Not someone else—only you.

So I decided to put myself into a personal rehab course—the best one I could construct while in this phase of rebirth. I had to create some self-worth if I was *ever* going to step up to the potential that had been bestowed on me at birth. If I was to create any shred of self-worth in my life, I had to take this rebirth on as a project. I needed to shut out any and all thoughts or opinions that said or even suggested otherwise. I certainly didn't do this perfectly by any means, yet I knew that it was something I needed to build on daily. I had to learn how to select what to shut out and whom to listen to. So it was a sort of filtering process that I needed to refine.

Life is a journey, not a destination.
—Steven Tyler

I did this through several steps, which I have placed here for you. I keep following through with these steps to be sure I am in a harmonious balance with my intentions for this life.

1. **Start from within.** Ignore any and all nonsupportive opinions, including those that come from your family or friends. Your opinion of yourself is the most important opinion of all. You know yourself better than anyone else does. Most of us have been hurt or let down by others at some point in life. It is essential NOT to internalize that abuse or let them continue to hurt us, because to do so is to relive that situation over and over. All the emotions and energies from that moment keep recurring as if it happened yesterday, and they will stop you from growing. If we let go of the past, ignore hurtful energy, and find a way to become grateful and happy, then *we* win. Take the time to tell yourself that you are a person worthy of happiness. And believe it! Make a list of all the things you like about yourself, and if you can't see anything yet, then make up a list of things you would like to be proud of in your life. If you have made mistakes that prevented you from believing that you are worthy of happiness, take measures to relieve that guilt: apologize to people you may have hurt, by talking, writing or praying; learn from those mistakes; and forgive all who may have hurt you. And most importantly, *forgive yourself.*

2. **Gain confidence by starting with the small things.** Start by taking small steps and making small choices. This will build your confidence in your ability to make good decisions. As you become secure in your ability to make good choices, you will gain confidence in yourself and become more secure in your ability to take on bigger things.

3. **Don't always try to please others.** It is wonderful if you are considerate of others, but think before sacrificing your own needs just to please someone else. It's completely rational to

want to help a loved one or a friend, especially if that person can contribute something to your life. But just consider that you may need to say no if your help to them is draining you. Being exhausted leaves us vulnerable, and then we start making decisions that we end up regretting. Become assertive and say no when you need to. Don't allow others to use you. Think of ways to make every situation a win-win. Take care of yourself.

4. **Avoid negative people.** People who have lower energy tend to infect you with their beliefs and are not giving you what is best for you. Don't compare yourself to others. Just be the best you can be while consistently improving along the way. Spend as little time as possible around people who are always complaining, or ask them to stop complaining around you.

5. **Face your fears and learn from your mistakes.** We fail only when we do not make the best of adversity. When something doesn't go the way you would have liked, you can always learn and grow from it, and that knowledge and growth will help the next time you're in a similar situation. The winners are the ones who get up after something knocks them down, so be a winner—get back up and go at it again.

6. **Stop the negative thoughts.** Whatever we believe about ourselves, whether it is the truth or utter rubbish, *becomes* the truth. This is what is known as a self-fulfilling prophecy. If we are consistently giving ourselves negative self-talk or thinking that we will never achieve success, this will be the energy we live in—in this case, a very *low vibration*. If, on the other hand, you make a habit of desiring an empowering energy through stating the possibilities you intend to bring to this life, you are turning this self-fulfilling prophecy to your advantage.

7. **Improve your self-confidence.** You can achieve this by doing things that make you feel good, doing them well, and desiring to do them better. Now go at it with the intention of improving

some, even if it's just a tiny bit. This will always give you a feeling of worth and gratification. Accomplishment is the key ingredient to building self-confidence. Just do it. And while you're at it, enjoy yourself.

8. **Do something to impress yourself.** Volunteer somewhere— say, at an animal shelter or a local food bank. Become a Big Brother or Big Sister. Help someone else. Nothing makes you feel a greater sense of worth than seeing how your help can make someone else's life a little smoother. Take a class to learn something new or to gain a skill that has always interested you. It could be an art class, CPR, a martial art, photography—the only limit is your imagination. Do something adventurous, so you can pounce on your fears or live out a childhood dream. Go scuba diving, rock climbing, or bungee jumping (professionally supervised, of course). Whenever a low-vibrational thought comes knocking, brush it off as you might an annoying fly, and get out and do some more dream building. Imagine how it would feel to complete your passion. You can raise your self-worth and grow it into part of your character.

9. **Don't try to be "perfect."** Perfection is different things to different people. No one is perfect in the eyes of everyone else, so by trying to be perfect, we're sure to set ourselves up for failure and disappointment. Instead, seek to be inspired and to *be yourself.*

10. **Learn to appreciate yourself.** We all have strengths, weaknesses, habits, and principles that define who we are and that make our energy distinctive. Spend more time focusing on qualities you like, and less on the ones you dislike.

11. **Reward yourself when you succeed.** Don't be afraid to bask in the glory of your successes. You deserve to feel the life of your intentions and revel in bringing them to life. When you believe in yourself completely, others will believe and trust in you. When you accomplish something you were aiming for, always

celebrate the accomplishment by treating yourself to something wonderful.

Throughout my rebirth, I kept my attention on what I needed to hear, and (most of the time, anyway) off what was said to me or around me that had no constructive intent. This kept me in an advancing mind-set and well positioned to take continuous forward action during the daunting rehabilitation process. And I continue to look into every situation and see how I can learn from it and in what ways I may better myself. I know I am on an eternal journey of self-empowerment and self-growth.

I would never have put the countless hours into creating this book or doing speaking engagements if I didn't value who I am and who I am becoming.

> *You are what you are and where you are because of what has gone into your mind. You can change what you are and where you are by changing what goes into your mind.*
> —**Zig Ziglar**

Exercise

Take a few minutes to read through all the steps again. They are the personal journey I had to take to get me this far. I know that each time I read them over periodically; they help me keep moving forward. Print the steps out so you can take them with you and have them in front of you anytime you want. Read them through and contemplate each step before taking action. Take these steps seriously and purposefully, and they will make a significant difference in your world.

ACTION

Chapter 26

I deas are just ideas unless you act on them. You didn't really believe that because you have a thought, it should become reality without any action on your part, did you?

For instance, let's say you want a new home. And yet, you have never put up pictures, talked about it with anyone, gone out to see one of the new model homes, or attended an open house in the neighborhood you wish to live in or near. Well, it should come as no great shock that you are no closer to that home you dream of than you were the first time you thought of it.

Now, let's say you want that same new house, but this time you've taken a very different approach. You've talked about the house in detail to anyone and everyone, gone out to see the house in person, not just in a photo, took the open-house walk-through, and *felt* the house physically and emotionally. You have brought that new home so close to you, you actually vibrate with the energy of its creation. You just need to reach out and bring it home mentally and emotionally, then give free rein to your *thoughts and emotions* of the joy you will begin to experience when you have the house. **Stop.** Take a moment and embrace your feelings completely. This will draw the house closer to your reality. This "casting of intent" has an especially powerful impact if you do it just before you lie down to rest. Within the next forty-eight hours, follow up these thoughts with walking through an open house or display home. You are reeling that new home in just as if it were a fish on the line.

> ***All you are seeking is seeking you***
> ***right back with the same intensity.***
> **—Bob Proctor**

As you begin not only to think about your cherished goal but also to take action on your thoughts, you will ingrain those thoughts into yourself. And soon they will become an empowering part of your character.

Think on something enough, and eventually you will initiate the thought of action. Maybe you can watch a program or presentation about the thing you want to do or have, or visit a showroom or a gallery where you can see it or touch it or take it out for a test drive.

Stop right now and look at what and who is around you. Now ask yourself, *Is this what I truly want?* Do what you can do today. Focus your time and energy, and take action on what you can do today. And do it well. Concern yourself with tomorrow when it comes. (It will.) Change your environment by taking action today.

Example

Crystal Andrus is a worldwide leader in the field of self-discovery and personal transformation. Crystal had a challenging start, with all kinds of childhood trauma, including sexual abuse and moving out when she was only 15. Then she became a divorced single mother of two beautiful girls. A little over a decade ago, Crystal stepped up to the challenge of finding herself. She went on a journey to seek out the beautiful woman she knew she was, who had been buried long ago. She started with her health. Crystal's journey began with a run. At first, she couldn't run farther than a few houses away, but she didn't quit—she kept exercising and learning new ways to be healthier. She discovered the magnificent woman she had always known was in there, and to her amazement, she found someone even greater than she expected.

Crystal has done well with what she learned while facing tough challenges that could easily have made her a victim. Instead, she decided to transform her knowledge from this journey into a teaching platform, where now her mission is to guide people to discover their hidden talents. Along with finding herself, she has found a new walk in life: she works with people in many areas of life, getting them on track and living at their best.

Crystal is now one of Canada's most influential health experts and motivational speakers. She can be seen and heard speaking regularly on television, radio, and at conventions and expos around North America. She is on TV regularly and conducts retreats and courses on personal and business development. Crystal is known all over the world through the hit show *X-Weighted* and has shared the stage with some of the most influential people of our time, including Dr. Wayne Dyer, Barbara Walters, Louise Hay, and the duchess of York, to name but a few.

Crystal decided to take action, serving others who either have endured a similar challenge or are stuck somewhere in their lives and can't find a way to break free and move on. In her personal journey, she made the decision to change, just as all the other leaders described in this book have done. They step up and face the trauma or challenge at hand and choose gratitude over grumbling, can-do over chaos. They have met challenges, and in the process of overcoming them, they found ways to come back and serve others. All the people in this book have found a way to have their trauma serve them, and in the process, they managed to design ways to serve many through their healing process. Helping others is yet another way of healing. They have chosen to learn and grow from all they have experienced, and then to share their lessons and knowledge with you and me, so that we can learn from them and fulfill our own life's purpose.

Instead of being a slave to a "bad" event,
become the master of it and have it serve you.

Experience

When I was a toddler, my mom would put me in a baby walker and let me wander around the house. My grandparents had wooden floors, and the walker was like an Indy car on the smooth, fast surface. I was 6 months young and ripping around like Mario Andretti on his own private racetrack. My parents had safety gates, of course, to keep the young speed racer confined to the track. One of the safety gates had just enough space for the adults to slip through, though not enough for the walker. Safe—or so they thought. Leave it to Daniel to find a way. I came burning my slippers off across the living room floor, hiked my walker up, cranked it sideways, and squeezed through the gated area. As my mom glanced my way I suddenly turned into Evil Knievel. Before she could grab me, I was doing a no-hands stair gap jump in my walker. I launched and cleared six steps and made a clean landing on my face. This was only the beginning of *Daredevil Dan,* volume 1.

It sounds amazing, but I am proud to say, I came away unscathed. That moment left me with the conviction that I can and will walk away from whatever comes my way. Injury after injury, hospitalization after hospitalization, I felt as though nothing could slow me down from doing whatever I wished, whether in sports or in business. If I was passionate enough about it and had enough intention, nothing stopped me from achieving my objective.

So at 29 years of age, I took test ride on a motorcycle I wanted to buy. Again, I was invincible and indestructible… right? Nothing could get in the way of my having a fantastic ride on that beautiful day. The only thing that could stop me or put me in harm's way—and did!—was my thoughts.

*Our thoughts determine the way we live. Our way of doing
things is a direct result of our way of thinking about things.*
—**Wallace D. Wattles**

I had businesses. I had friends. I had great health, and a life that was
developing into the life I had always dreamed about (with, of course,
the odd bump here and there). So why, you may ask, did I get into
this life-changing incident? Are you ready for this? (Because it's an eye
opener!) Looking back on my life, I realized that it had been leading up
to this for a long time. One fall after another, one surgery after another,
I had lived under the impression that I was indestructible. Yes, I may
have got a break or bump, but I always came back stronger, better, faster
than before. To my way of thinking, nothing could slow me down or
take me out of the race to accomplish all I wanted. With this mind-set,
I stepped blithely into harm's way time after time, thinking nothing
could stop me.

When I went in and picked up the bike, I had been thinking of all
I couldn't afford to lose: *I don't need another injury—an accident would
really suck. It would all lead to a devastating outcome, losing my companies,
and letting my clients and friends down. I would place myself in a position
of not being able to ride my bike hard, as I love to do, not being in the
next film my friend is producing, not getting to participate in the upcoming
cross-country bike race, not getting to follow through with my passion of
designing, building, and renovating homes.* So you see where my mind
and thoughts were: on all that could go wrong, not to mention wrecking
a brand-new bike. I certainly was not focused on a wonderful ride in the
country, with a gorgeous, scenic view and glorious weather. Instead, my
mind was lost down a destructive trail.

The question is, why or how did this incident happen? I have to say,
I called it all into my life.

These days, my thoughts and focus are on creative intentions as I
move forward. I will benefit as much as I can from what I have learned
along this journey of re-creation. I learn from other leaders who share

their knowledge and experience through their different programs and events. I am creating my wealth and my worth, and I choose my own thoughts! This is my life! I want to live it the way *I* intend it to be.

Exercise

There are actions you can take on anything you can dream of, anything you intend for this life: a house, a soul mate, vital health, or perhaps a new career and financial freedom. Whether it's the very first baby steps or something you have known for a long time that you must follow through on, your focus in this exercise is on *action*. Take it now. Follow through with your intentions. *Claim your right* to this life! Whatever steps you didn't do while reading this book, now is the time. Go back and do them. Your intention in reading this book was to undergo a change that would let you express yourself and manifest your being. My intentions are to have you unlock and put to use the hidden treasures that are buried within you, so that you can enjoy a life you are proud to remember and to share with others.

Chapter 27

LIVING
YOUR WORD

S teven Siebold has a powerful message of how living your word changes your life and the lives of others around you. I enjoy listening to him often, because his message has made a difference in my life. And I believe it will make a difference in yours. The next few paragraphs are part of his message to all of us.

You are a person of your word, and your handshake seals the deal. You always do what you say you're going to do. You are someone people can count on, and everyone around you knows it. When you commit to something or someone, you always come through. Your attitudes and behaviors are solid at all times. People always know what to expect when they interact with you. This is why people gravitate to you. You're always upbeat, positive, and inspiring. You always know what to say or where to direct people to get their inspiration, knowing that through your contact you will leave them with a feeling of increase. Friends and family always come to you when they need a new vision on the situation. This is because you're a creative conversationalist and problem solver. The most powerful attribute you possess is that you can always find greatness and see the gifts in others. You have a tremendous willingness to see others' potential and the power they carry. You yearn to enrich others, to draw out their potential and empower them to put it to good use. You live your word out regularly.

> *Fools live to regret their words,*
> *wise men to regret their silence.*
> **—Will Henry**

Watch the words you cast at others, for they will and do become you. The greatness you see in others will be seen in you. You are a master at finding the good in any situation. This is why your family and friends always look to you for your thoughts on their situations. You are a person of integrity. This is why people trust you and want to befriend you. It is said that your actions speak louder than your words, so if you are living your word, your actions are speaking your word. Then you are becoming a person whom others can count on, and they believe that all you speak on will be achieved. Your life is the proof, for it is as you have designed it to be.

Example

Have you ever met someone who hasn't used the word "no" in years? I have. Her name is Yvonne Oswald, and she is a U.S. national award-winning pioneer in the personal growth field, nominated in 2008 by the Coalition of Visionary Resources for her unique CD *Mind Magic*. She grew up in an environment where words got a lot of use as negative tools. But when her daughter was born, Yvonne decided she wanted to raise her in a positive, constructive environment, and because she understands the power of words, she decided to clear the word "no" from her vocabulary, especially when with her daughter. Instead of "no," she taught her *possibilities*. Luck seems to follow the young girl around. Yvonne says that her daughter's friends called her "the luckiest girl," because she was raised with powerful positive words and a constructive mind-set. Yvonne's daughter knows that she can accomplish anything she desires, just as Paulo Coehlo wrote in *The Alchemist:* "…when you want something, all the universe conspires in helping you to achieve it." As so can you! All you need do is undress from all those limiting clothes you've been carrying for years, which have outlived their usefulness. Then, when the opportunity arises for you to shine, you'll be ready.

Action makes more fortune than caution.
—Luc DeClapiers

Yvonne's message is that words are powerful. She brings to our attention how the meanings of words change through time and how, for example, the word "positive" is not as positive as we may think. If you are diagnosed as "positive" for an illness, it means you are sick. So the word's connotation is not exclusive to the domain of things that are good. As you become aware of your language, you will notice the number of words that you can replace with high-energy words, to give you improved results. Get someone (Yvonne recommends getting a Switch™ buddy) to help you change the words, by saying "Switch!" every time they hear you say a low-energy word. There is also the word "but," which completely negates everything that was said before it. How many times have you talked about something you want and followed your statement with a "but"? What message is the universe receiving from you? Remember, the universe conspires to help you achieve what you want. Your job is to send the universe a clear and loud message of what you DO want.

Words affect our emotions as well. You will notice this if you are talking with someone who is sad or complaining, or if *you* are the one who is talking about sadness or complaining about something. The words have a vibration, and they will change the vibration of your surroundings. From now on, mind *every single word* that comes out of you through your voice, writing, or thoughts; and every word that comes toward you through your ears and eyes. They are truly powerful!

Yvonne has become a living example of how any person can live life fully and manifest it to match their expectations. What she has accomplished and who she has become have their foundation in her *thoughts* because, as we now know, our thoughts become things through our words and actions. Her powerful commitment to transforming, uplifting, and energizing her clients and whomever she attracts has become her purpose in life. Yvonne's intentions of fulfilling her purpose in this world have led her to study and practice so she can follow through on her commitment to transform lives.

Experience

The motorcycle crash knocked the loose marbles in my head into a more useful order—well, at least in most areas (as my family will attest). As I found that I could be counted on and trusted, many doors were opened, and along with guidance came help. Once your family, friends, and public see greatness in you, your words will seal the deal. You are now held accountable for all that flows out of your mouth, and for your actions that follow. It is not an easy task, especially when we are accustomed to changing our mind often or saying things we don't mean. We have to decide to make a commitment to *constant and never-ending improvement.*

I have been promoted and followed through my progress in rehab and through the speaking circuit. It is amazing who calls, who e-mails, who appears in my life at just about any place or time of day. When I ask how and where they heard of me, it almost always comes down to someone who trusted me because they knew my word was good. I know that if I am to request and achieve outstanding outcomes in my life, I must compare myself to the best. I don't dare compare myself to the merely average. If I focused only on the average, I would get only average results. I crave the best results for my life, so I must focus on the best.

I intend to be of service for the medical/rehabilitation communities around the world. An intention and passion of this magnitude will promote me to take steps only in that direction, to bring fulfillment and carry out my purpose for this life. I will share with and talk to people whom many lack the confidence to approach.

So if my intention is to become the best at what I do, this must bring out the best in me and draw me closer to my visions, allowing me to walk in a higher vibration, attracting like energy my way, and pushing me constantly to improve myself. If I intend to walk with the great leaders in the industry, I must be studying them, following their footsteps, comparing my actions to their actions, and raising my standards continuously. If I am doing this, I am becoming *all I think on and speak on.*

> *You cannot always control what goes on outside,*
> *but you can control what goes on inside.*
> **—Wayne Dyer**

During the early stages of my rebirth, I collided with the wall of frustration. I thought I was not making any headway in developing my new life. I was feeling stagnant, tired, and worn out.

It is these moments of self-doubt, when we appear not to be making any headway and feel as though we are running in circles, that prove to us that we are changing old, unwanted habits and stretching ourselves into a new life. As long as you have honestly been attempting to progress in your venture, there is always forward motion, whether you see it or not. Often, it is when you think and feel that you are your wasting time that you are actually making the most progress. These times are the training or foundation for future steps in your quest. Anytime I experienced these moments of self-doubt, I found that an abundance of opportunities accompanied the struggle as long as I pushed strong and long enough.

Exercise

When you say you are going to do something, stop for a moment and understand how much this could mean to somebody and how much it could benefit them when you follow through. Understand how much it will mean to *you*. From now on, when you say you are going to do something, do it, no matter what! Make it happen, because when you make a promise with your words, your honor is at stake. Even if no one around you is holding themselves to their word, you are different. Your word is gold. This exercise holds you to a higher standard. This could be your gift. You are a creative spirit, and you manifest whatever you think on. This is where you consciously begin to manifest your intentions. Write out what you have said you're going to do or want to do, and read it when you wake up, at every meal, and before you call it a night. Call it into action, and you will be amazed at what you begin to attract in this life.

Chapter 28

SUCCESS

*The secret of success lies in forming the habit
of doing things that failures don't like to do.*
—Bob Proctor

There is no hidden secret to succeeding in life. Succeeding is about consciously deciding to continue when the average person might give up. You don't need to know *how* you will achieve your dreams. You just need to know that you will—the how always appears. Walk forward with total faith, purpose, gratitude, and intention, and the how will appear at the right time. As you begin to manifest your life, people and opportunities will come to you with the key, teachings, or opportunity that allows you to continue your journey and accomplish your goal.

Believe that it will happen, and the how will appear.

The keys and messages will show up in your life. People will appear. You will be introduced to ways of acquiring knowledge that you never knew existed. You will think differently. You will act, talk, and move in ways that promote others to ask you what you're up to. The initial step in developing any success is the choice to feel it all, even before you manifest it in the material world. As we have said, *you become what you think about all day long,* so if you're thinking success, you will adopt the ways of being that fit the desire you intend. This means switching your mind off what you don't like and onto what you want to manifest. It begins with the feeling of success and believing that you are *whatever your imagination can create,* even if, in this moment, you are further than you have ever been from that desired state. You will eventually generate the actions and habits of the successful, and you will draw it all to you with the *law of attraction.* People will get curious about what you're doing and where you're going, and as if by magic, doors will open and opportunities will appear. All is brought to you by action, and it is through gratitude that you will receive it.

Any champion or leader in this world gets things accomplished by taking action, and to take action one must put the will to work. They also have a support system they have built—something akin to a mastermind group. When you have in your chosen field the support of a team of like-minded people shooting for the same or similar objectives, you begin to take not just steps but *leaps.* This happens to be one of the pillars in wealth dynamics. It is a big part of why "the rich get richer." When they have support and a confident leader they move ahead. Even when you fall or make mistakes, your support team stands with you on your walk, supporting you and nudging you along. As you gather this support team, you will find that you are moving in a higher energy frequency.

Example

When Brendon Burchard was 19, just after his freshman year of college, he went to the Dominican Republic and was working a summertime job. This is where he discovered greatness in himself and embarked on a new life, a successful life. After going through a dramatic experience, he suddenly had a choice to make. He could fight and return to life, living fully, loving completely, and making a difference, or he could fall down and give up on himself and the world.

Brendon was blessed, for at that moment his spirit realized that there was a higher reason for him to be alive. Brendon says that his book *Life's Golden Ticket* is about starting anew, helping people understand that they have a choice and a chance to wake up and be passionate about life again without having to slog through all the fears of loss.

Brendon Burchard is one of the most successful and inspirational people I have ever had the pleasure to meet. When I first met him in 2007, he inspired me to follow my dreams and my purpose. I was impressed by his drive to move forward in life, his endless creativity, how he stretched the limits to accomplish the unimaginable, and how he redefined the way professionals connect with the world through their businesses. He also guides and teaches others to become better by paying forward the lessons he has learned. He knows that by helping others grow, he will grow at the same time. Most importantly, he learned that he can live a dream life at a youthful and vibrant age, with a whole lifetime ahead to experience it!

Remember what I was telling you about the creative mind? Brendon has demonstrated over and over again that by having a creative mind, you can become successful beyond your wildest dreams and do just about anything you can imagine. It isn't really about the financial profit; it's about the spiritual and emotional payoff of being a witness to the success of those you have helped in achieving their dreams. Your sense of fulfillment will certainly be much bigger if your goals include a physical, a mental, a spiritual, and an emotional component. That way, you will get to savor many different joys of this life. Brendon has helped make a better world by reaching thousands of people and helping them lead a happier, more fulfilled life by achieving all the many components of success.

> *When you stand on the edge of the light of what you know, one of two things will happen with your faith: you will find a strong place to stand, or you will fly!*
> —**Brendon Burchard**

Brendon has a very strong faith—something we all need in order to move forward in life. As you learn more about successful people like Brendon, you come to realize that they all had to face a moment—or many moments—when faith made all the difference in their lives. You, too, will need to walk, or maybe jump, into the unknown with the certainty that every step you are taking will bring you closer to your goal.

Experience

I always knew I had a greater mission in life to fulfill. I kept getting those nudges from our Creator about what I should be doing with my time here. Well, I kept ignoring those nudges, and they began to get stronger and stronger as time went on, until I had no choice but to listen to the divine force showing me what I needed to do and how I should go about doing it.

Success: this is a word that hit every point on the scale during my journey, from learning to walk to running. I learned from everything I have been writing about in this book and from all the examples I have been giving you. From these examples and my own trial and error, I am where I am today, in a state of *constant and never-ending improvement.* The success I wish to share—the greatest thing I have done so far—is my re-creation after the incident.

You now know the story of my rebirth. The biggest success of it all, I have to say, is my feeling of a newfound faith in the omnipotence of our Creator. I have had wonderful success in connecting with higher-energy-inducing healing and growth in this body. I know that I will have many more successes to rejoice in as this life plays out, and the greatest success of them all is learning how to live life and create a future for myself after all I have journeyed through.

I am now walking very well and almost running. I am speaking at many different events, on multiple topics, and the main message is that we all have an infinite store of human potential, the purpose of our intentions, and the power of our mind. The exciting part of all this is that I have not yet experienced my biggest success, for I know that success is ever expanding and always opening more doors along the way.

I have been blessed with the opportunity to speak in some of the finest medical schools and hospitals in Canada. I share with my audiences the spiritual journey I have taken, especially what I have learned about the human potential and the psychic laws behind finding the hidden talents and gifts we all have been blessed with. I also go speak to high school audiences about the purpose of intention and the power of the mind-set, where it can and will lead you—whether you're paying attention to it or not. I get to do what I always dreamed of doing, because I am sharing the lessons I've learned during this journey.

> *True success is when you feel great about who*
> *you are, what you do, and what you have.*
> **—Yvonne Oswald**

I intend to help guide you and to give you ways to overcome adversity with greater ease, enjoyment, and fulfillment. That in itself is a WIN.

Exercise

This exercise brings together everything you have just used. What you have learned throughout the journey of this book, you can *apply it all* here. Look at the life you have created thus far. Look at anything you have done to guide, help, support, facilitate, or promote someone else's growth—such as by being a parent, guardian, supervisor, coach, or teammate. If what you have done has benefited you or someone else, you have succeeded with your intention.

Now, knowing what you know, having fine-tuned and expanded your life through the exercises in this book, you know how you can apply these to your future endeavors. So here is your next step: apply daily all that you have learned through this book, and share with others your experiences and knowledge so they, too, can grow with you. Go on and live the life of your choice!

ABOUT THE AUTHOR

 **Daniel Bax is an inspirational** speaker and breakthrough strategist and coach for the medical industry and for nonprofit organizations dedicated to helping people with acquired brain injury. Since Daniel recovered his voice and body movement, he has been traveling across North America, sharing his inspiring story. He has been invited to talk to doctors, therapists, technicians, and health-care personnel at hospitals, nonprofits, and private companies that provide support and health-care services.

Daniel is a yearly guest speaker to first-year naturopathic medicine students at the Canadian College of Naturopathic Medicine in Ontario, the third most recognized naturopathic medicine school in North America. He is also on the panel of experts that, each year, help evaluate and provide feedback to occupational therapy and physical therapy students at the School of Rehabilitation Science at McMaster University. This is one of the leading teaching institutions in Canada, whose teachers are acknowledged nationally and internationally as leaders in occupational therapy and physiotherapy research.

For the past four years, Daniel has been invited to speak to Community and Hospital Against Trauma (CHAT). This is a unique awareness program run by the Trauma Program at the General Hospital in Hamilton, Ontario, which introduces young adults to potential injury and risk-related behaviors.

Daniel has been the keynote speaker for Sun Life Insurance and at the Neurological Rehabilitation Institute of Ontario during its Breakfast Meetings, where rehabilitation therapists and other professionals serving the industry receive continuing education. He speaks on human potential and the importance of communication between the professionals and their clients.

Currently, Daniel is assisting Elements Support Service in developing its newest project, e-Rehab. Elements Support Service offers rehabilitation services for people with brain injury or other serious trauma. Its new division uses the latest technological advances to provide a unique service designed to support people who experience cognitive impairments and executive dysfunction.

Now, as an author, Daniel will reach thousands of people as he fulfills his life's purpose of bringing his uplifting message and guidance to all who are ready to redirect their life and transform it into the life of their choice.